A woman's guide to **BUSINESS DOMINATION**

Real-life wisdom from empowered women who wanted more

Compiled by
ANNIE GIBBINS

Copyright © Annie Gibbins

First published in Australia in 2022
by KMD Books
Waikiki, WA 6169

All rights reserved. No part of this book may be used or reproduced by any means, graphic, electronic, or mechanical, including photocopying, recording, taping or by any information storage retrieval system without the written permission of the copyright owner except in the case of brief quotations embodied in critical articles and reviews.

Because of the dynamic nature of the Internet, any web addresses or links contained in this book may have changed since publication and may no longer be vaild. The views expressed in this work are solely those of the author and do not necessarily reflect the views of the publisher and the publisher hereby disclaims any responsibility for them.

 A catalogue record for this work is available from the National Library of Australia

National Library of Australia Catalogue-in-Publication data:

A Woman's Guide to Business Domination/Annie Gibbins

ISBN:
978-0-6455691-5-5
(Paperback)

ISBN:
978-0-6455691-6-2
(Ebook)

CONTENTS

FOREWORD
Hazel Herrington 1

EXECUTING YOUR GROWTH STRATEGY
Annie Gibbins 3

DELIVERING EXEMPLARY CUSTOMER SERVICE
Angela Schutz 25

BREAKING THROUGH IMPOSTER SYNDROME
Annette Densham 39

WHY SEGMENTING YOUR MARKET SMALLER MAKES FOR BIGGER BUSINESS
Ayumi Uyeda 51

LETTING YOUR MISSION GUIDE YOUR STRATEGY
Babita Spinelli 69

CREATING A UNIQUE VALUE PROPOSITION
Dr Adama Kalokoh 88

LEVERAGING TECHNOLOGY TO DOMINATE THE BUSINESS ECOSYSTEM
Dr Ingrid Vasiliu-Feltes 104

HOW DOES YOUR BRAIN HEALTH AFFECT YOUR BUSINESS SUCCESS?
Dr Isabel Bertran-Hunsinger MD 127

BREAKING THE GLASS CEILING FOR WOMEN OF COLOUR IN MEDICAL LEADERSHIP
Dr M Talat Uppal 142

CEO BRANDING FOR SUCCESS
Hazel Herrington 153

SHOWING UP AS YOUR AUTHENTIC SELF
Jane Vandermeer 165

CREATING A JOB YOU LOVE FROM THE GROUND UP
Karen McDermott 182

THE POWER OF CONNECTION
Leezá Carlone Steindorf 194

MARKET DEVELOPMENT
Linda Fisk 209

INSIGHTS INTO WHY CONSUMERS BUY FROM YOU
Naila Qazi 227

LEVERAGING INTELLECTUAL PROPERTY RIGHTS
Pooja Bhatia 241

FIND YOUR OWN WAY
Sarah Blake..*257*

HOW TO MAINTAIN MOMENTUM IN BUSINESS
Shelia Farr *276*

ANNIE'S JOURNEY OF BECOMING
Annie Gibbins..*287*

FOREWORD

Hazel Herrington

I am delighted to write the foreword for Annie Gibbins' new book, *A Woman's Guide to Business Domination*. This book is a powerful and timely reminder of the importance of women in the business world.

Women have always been the backbone of successful businesses, but too often their contributions have gone unnoticed or unacknowledged. This book is co-authored by some of the most powerful and influential women in business and is sure to be an inspiration to all who read it.

It shines a light on the successes of women in business and provides valuable advice for women who want to achieve business domination. As someone fortunate enough to work closely with Annie, I can attest to her incredible passion for helping women reach their full potential.

Annie is a tireless advocate for gender equality, and she has inspired countless women to pursue their dreams. I am confident that *A Woman's Guide to Business Domination* will have a similarly profound impact on its readers.

This book is essential reading for any woman who is serious about succeeding in business. I am honoured to have contributed the foreword, and I am excited to see the difference this book will make in the lives of its readers.

Thank you, Annie, for the opportunity to be a part of this important project.

EXECUTING YOUR GROWTH STRATEGY

Annie Gibbins

This book was created for a purpose: unite leaders globally, share experiences to inspire others and navigate strategically the path to success. Understanding the fundamentals has been covered in multiple books, so I don't see this anthology as another how-to guide, but a passion-filled and brilliantly executed collection of stories from women who matter. Women who have climbed the career ladder in adversity, women who have pushed their limits and challenged themselves and women who are unafraid to put their stories out there.

The empowering component and pinnacle core of *The Woman's Guide to Business Domination* is diversity, versatility and difference. For so long, women have been herded into categories, boxes and drop-down menus in order to fit. The irony is, we champion young women and girls to see themselves as unique and different. We hope that the next generation of future women will live in a society that promotes difference and individuality. However, change seems to be either regressive or sluggishly progressive. So, when I gathered my fleet of writers, my only caveat was 'be different'.

Everyone has a backstory, and it's our backstory that makes our brand stand out. Whether you are a tech-head in a corporate conglomerate, an academic with a passion for learning or a person who has overcome tragedy beyond comprehension, it's our story that counts.

Our story often operates in direct correlation to our worth. How we see ourselves is not always how others perceive us. How we communicate our message doesn't always hit the mark. How we thrive doesn't always match a typical pathway. However, there is only one of us, and we must remember, in order to grow, we must understand that we are the experts of our experiences. It is in these experiences that we will grow our strategy, mark our brand and become leaders in the way that we always hoped to be.

Get up close and personal with your fear

It's simple but true: mindset matters. Did you know, the human brain processes approximately ninety thousand thoughts per day? How we direct our attitude will be cemented by each of those thoughts. If your tank is running on red or your belief system is 'my life is a glass half empty', then you are cementing failure after failure.

As a leader, I have learnt to see failures as future wins. Without them, we don't learn, stretch or grow. We need this process to do a better job next time. To be leaders, we need to innovate, and we all know any invented prototype rarely works on the first go. So, get ready to become more tenacious because seeing a failure and believing we are failures are juxtaposed perspectives.

As an advocate for education, I encourage my children, teams, organisation and clients to keep learning. 'Never close a book or turn off a podcast if valuable information is being absorbed,' I often remark. But education is only part of the jigsaw puzzle as our mindset and limiting beliefs are constantly at play in the background. We need to continually work on exploring our unconscious mind as often we aren't even aware that we are betting for a bad day.

To succeed in business, here are some key tips and tricks that helped me along the way:

Seek out positive influences
Intentionally seeking out positive influences or people in your life is paramount to creating a kickass mindset. When you start interacting in an environment that inspires, equips and empowers you to rise, you will achieve what you thought was previously impossible. They will teach you how to dream big and act bigger.

Swim with the tide
Many of us, at times, feel like we are swimming against the tide, which is exhausting and takes effort that is better spent elsewhere. To go with the flow, you need to find workable solutions instead of resisting change. It can feel scary and make you feel uncomfortable, however, when you push through and learn to ride a new wave, you may find situations that have been designed perfectly for you to learn, grow and triumph.

Strive to be positive
Positive people bring joy, happiness and uplifting energy, plus they are fun to be around, and what's not to love about

that?! While it's not realistic to be positive all the time, it is possible most of the time. It is how we respond to situations that matters and you can do this with a positive attitude while feeling the depth of your emotions and remaining wise and responsive to risk. When you start looking closely, there are positives to find in almost every situation, even the challenging ones. Once you shift your mindset towards 'how can I help?' or 'what can I do?', you will become more motivated to lean into your true potential.

Don't forget you are dealing with humans
Our emotional intelligence is not emotional, and we need it more than ever. Modern business requires us to connect with people in a personal way as we are measured by how we respond to their specific needs. As leaders, we need to inspire and not just venture on a one-woman journey to the bank. Whilst the bottom line is everything, humanness is needed more than ever. So, as you juggle, create, sell and manage, try to engage a leadership style that embraces collective thought, engagement and ownership. Together we achieve more.

It's not the role, it's the ambition that counts

There is a misconception that leadership is a 'look' rather than a concept. Often, when people think of female leadership, they envisage a woman standing at the helm of the boardroom, in a power suit, commanding the room. Whilst this image is certainly one I love, it's also grossly incorrect. See this is a stereotype – another cookie-cutter ideal of women in power.

The spin I want to put on this assumption is that a hairdresser, beautician, restaurateur or property developer can be a female leader. Gone are the days of briefcases, wall-to-wall desks and

Filofaxes (seriously, are they even making them anymore?).

The conventional corporate queen can be literally anything.

With our digital footprint measuring success via impressions, insights and clicks-per-view, success is about 'profiling' versus 'profile'. In fact, I love coaching and empowering my clients in any industry. This not only helps them as startups, scaleups or dominators in their business access to me, but I in turn learn from them. I research the sector, scout out the competition and devise progressive business strategies that align with their visions and not the pre-pandemic landscape.

In a recent article published by [1]Statista, it was reported that in the financial year 2020, over 344,000 new businesses entered the Australian market. By the end of that financial year, there were over 2.42 million businesses operating in Australia. Whilst the majority of these successful startups were technology focused, the products ranged from fashion to travel. I see it as my responsibility to never shy away from digital evolution, because that is the direction we are heading.

Take your dream, carve it carefully, lean into and learn the digital trends.

Know your *why*

Not one to take the slow lane, I am driven by dismantling the glass ceiling and removing the invisible barriers to success that many women come up against in their business and life journey.

Essentially, I am a leader that wants to expose the potential of those passionate for transformation. [2]Understanding how to frame business formulas, strategies and operational plans is only half the hurdle. So many of life's big answers exist in natural-born leaders,

---

1) statista.com/topics/4729/start-ups-in-australia/?fbclid=IwAR3d4IiRiPz5dvUJ65xUxiK2qcIY iN2F_e_UwtGcNWWM7qCNdpFJ2SVQOqQ#topicHeader__wrapper
2) ncbi.nlm.nih.gov/pmc/articles/PMC4853380

but when there is a lack of confidence and clarity to uncover them single-handedly, imposter syndrome comes knocking. According to a research study conducted by Frontiers in Psychology, they concluded the importance of recognising 'the interplay between coaches' leadership behaviours and coaches' experiences and needs during the coaching process'. This would suggest the significant importance of my overarching desire to integrate my life experience with my current coaching model.

Emerging from a global pandemic is going to challenge our economy more than ever. Behind every conglomerate on a mission is a woman with a dream. My ultimate dream is to empower women to thrive – and not just survive – with conviction, gumption and passion for a better day.

Throughout my life, I have taken many leaps into the unknown. As they say, 'If fear didn't exist what would you do?' Many of us are governed by fears, and legitimate ones at that. Being an entrepreneur isn't just about ambition, it's layered with risk. Risk that the finances won't stack up, that people won't back your product and perhaps you're not the leader you believe yourself to be. Therefore, starting a side-hustle is not for the faint-hearted, but when you make the decision to give your brand a go, you are opening the doors to limitless success.

I think it's also important to define what a side-hustle is. More than ever, people are tapping into the digital landscape to explore a new career, education and opportunity. If you are not online these days, you are almost doomed because the world has migrated virtually. When the world closed its borders at the beginning of the pandemic, so many of us transitioned to remote everything. We got a taster of what life could look like without high-rise offices and daily commute. And do you know? It worked.

Budding 'intrapreneurs' were seeing how much success was

available at the touch of a button (literally). Whilst borders were closing, the world was opening. People were dusting off back-burner businesses and dabbling in the idea of launching their startup alongside their full-time professional role. For the first time in history, a disconnected world was more in-tune than ever.

We are asking the big life questions: *Is this the job I want to do forever? If I don't change my goals now, when will I? What is my happiness worth?* Across the globe, dissatisfied workers were questioning everything and anything about the future they wanted. They identified their needs from their wants, and most wanted a new beginning.

So, my final message to you is: dare to dream. Dare to dream in ways you never thought you could. Achieve those dreams, but employ a team of supporters around you. Success is hard work. Success can be lonely. Success doesn't come without risk. However, the only thing worse than work, fear and risk, is regret.

Be the CEO of your life, the hero in your story and the writer of your story.

I believe in you.

Own your dream

It always staggers me when I hear women apologise for wanting to be rich, like it's a dirty secret to be ashamed of. Over a girl-gang brunch, I listened to a conversation about life goals. 'Of course, she will always hope for health and happiness for those she loves,' one remarked. Another friend tentatively leaned into the group and said, 'I really want to be wealthy.' Immediately, my instinct was to high-five her ambition, but it all went deadly quiet. For me, I didn't understand why acknowledging worth through an exchange of money is a faux pas we should leave behind closed doors.

So, I am here to ensure that every woman has no hesitation about wanting a bank balance of her own. Financial independence brings freedom to make choices about the things that matter, and that is priceless. For some, it will require rewriting your money-mindset narrative, but once you do, there will be no stopping you.

For every financially successful female coach and/or entrepreneur, there are thousands who may be successful in the eyes of their grateful clients, but are simply not making anywhere near the income they would like.

Even if you're making a decent living and you can meet your monthly commitments, you may be feeling frustrated because there's little left to spare in your income. If there is no plan to realise those dreams you keep putting off, it's time for some changes.

Here are some of my top tips:

Define your money story
Your money story and relationship with money will play a big part on how you view it. Perhaps you were raised in a household with next to no income, or your family was wealthy and you wanted for nothing. Either way, how you view money, materialism and financial stability will stem from the parts you never quite realised. Instead of thinking, *I will never get to my goal*, reframe your doubt to, *One day, I am going to be a millionaire*. Sounds simple, right? It's because it can be. It doesn't really matter which type of negative money stories you have. If it leaves you feeling financially fearful and disempowered, it is a money story you need to change.

Give up the money ghosts
When you understand your money story and the limiting beliefs

associated with your spending habits, you can turn the tide on past habits. If you are a serial giver-upper, undercharge your clients or believe that money will not be assigned to your future, then it won't be. Narrative is everything when it comes to fundamental and solid change. By ridding the guilt, shame or negative opinion we have when it comes to making money, you stand a chance of creating the life you truly deserve.

Know your worth
So much of money is not about money making. It's about the value we place on ourselves. No-one will invest in your product, brand and even you, if you don't invest in yourself. Lose the money mishaps – overspending, underbilling and procrastinating – and believe that money is, in fact, not a stress, but your ticket to that seven-figure salary.

How to build a brand with purpose
'The brands that will thrive in the coming years are the ones that have a purpose beyond profit.' – Richard Branson

A purpose-driven brand is a brand that is motivated by their core mission. The reason they exist is to solve a problem or meet a need in society, and that purpose informs the brand's vision, mission, story, identity, decision-making and more.

While profit may not be the main driver, the reason behind the purpose fuels the momentum of the business, and that ensures its sustainability to continue making a difference!

Considering [3]63% of consumers prefer to purchase from purpose-driven brands, you are well positioned to be successful. Modern customers love to relate to a story they connect with and

---
3) accenture.com/us-en/insights/strategy/brand-purpose?c=strat_competitiveagilnovalue_10437227&n=mrl_1118

will team up to support you in your cause.

Never underestimate the value of bringing others on your journey. We all need and love long-term customers! Weave your purpose and passion into your business and make it integral to everything you do. Be creative with how you share your story and engage with your market. Business is more fun when there is active engagement. For example, I have had clients be the face of advertising campaigns and invited to participate in surveys or competitions. Remember, actions speak louder than words so make sure your clients see you practicing what you preach. They should feel a consistent energy coming from your brand, so aim to be consistent.

Coming from a background in health and education, I am passionate about providing interventions that promote wellness. While not every charity has the initial finance to make a tangible impact, when you combine purpose and passion with strong business principles, a magic formula starts to activate. Once you know how to effectively 'share the good news' you will find yourself attracting other prospects like bees to honey.

Currently, I hold multiple advisory roles on several boards, and my expertise to fundraise at both a national and international level has enabled so many causes to do what they do best: advocate. Now, many of my clients come to me with big ideas. They are successful businesswomen at senior executive levels, but they want to do more. Some have been touched personally by a trauma, whilst others simply have a desire to give back. The reason advocacy and activism exist is because they have discovered their *why*.

Identifying your *why* is key. In the world of advocacy, building from the ground up will establish your purpose. This could, in fact, apply to any ambition. But when we are in the thick of a business brainstorm, we don't always see the ideas that are often staring us in the face. I work with women ranging from startup devotees to CEOs on a seven-figure salary, but having an objective cheerleader in the room can transform a concept into a go-live brand.

Like anything, when you are creating a purpose, be it a relationship, a family or business, going back to basics is everything. I urge all women who read this to identify their purpose with conviction, evaluate its sustainability, create uplifting content, pitch their plan and connect with a powerhouse network who will never leave their side.

Like fear, myths about business have a nasty way of working themselves into a 'success-building bootcamp'. Much like the unhelpful download of fake news, there are many myths that catapult an idea into the 'too-hard basket'. Before we know it, we have parked our plans for growth and find ourselves back on the slow train we have been riding for years. Glossy magazines will always, and should, showcase the success stories that sell. But being an entrepreneur and woman in business can also be a calamity of errors.

As one of Australia's leading business influencers, I am here to tell you the myths that need debunking, and how to keep them exactly where they belong: in your desktop recycle bin.

I'm not a typical expert

You are the expert of your experiences. If you are ready to take the next step in building your success, trust that you have the skills and services needed at hand. No-one is going to be more passionate about your brand than you. And what you don't know, you will learn ... and fast. Every CEO, senior leader and global ambassador has learnt on the job and been one foot in front of their audience. But their biggest attribute is their instinct. Tap into that, and you will be your own expert in no time.

People won't buy from me when they have Google

We are a generation that needs 'instant everything'. We want a movie, we go to Netflix; we want a meal, we head to Uber Eats; we want love, we swipe on Tinder. Many have no patience or capacity to find the answers if it will take longer than five minutes. The compelling part of your brand is that you are delivering what Google cannot: 'hearty experience'. Universities do not focus on the curriculum like they did because any information found in a PowerPoint can now be found on the internet. Education institutions are now looking for something that cannot be found via SEO rankings – experience from the industry leaders and their powerful networks. Rather than competing with global juggernauts, go niche and collaborate with your available networks and resources.

There are brands out there like mine

This is a good thing! This means that you are on track. Now the task is discovering your uniqueness, your brand story and how you are going to tell it with originality and difference. The truth is almost every single problem worth solving has already been tackled. Blogs, books and online courses exist, but there is only one of you. What makes you and your brand a stand-out?

Entrepreneurs can predict the future

This is somewhat true, but this statement is more about confidence in a vision than an entrepreneur's ability to time travel. Entrepreneurs, startups and powerhouse business moguls have an innate ability to see a gap in the untapped market. They identify an investment, product or service unlike any other, but their manifestation can often be mistaken for prediction.

Going it solo is your only option
Wrong. Whilst entrepreneurs are visionary and appear to be solo flyers, they often rely on a suite of skills in the boardroom. As a coach, I champion my clients to believe in their wildest dreams. I lead a business where knowing the skills of my employees ensures I can do my job better, and in turn, the company will excel. Ego and entrepreneurship in healthy doses work, but having an idea without a partner means accountability and prosperity can fall by the wayside.

Business success is the only success
Success is defined by a set of values and standards only you can access. For some, success is a seven-figure salary, for others, it's becoming a CEO after twenty years as a 2IC, and for others still, it's to get back into the workforce after a ten-year gap whilst raising the family. As an advocate for gender equality, I am committed to ensuring all women and girls are included in any goal they set their sights on. It's our job as leaders to ensure diversity, and success is defined by the woman that makes it, and it's accessible to all.

Get a leg-up, not a handout
Female CEOs remain a rare commodity. And it's time for drastic change. Certainly, we are seeing more women filling executive leadership roles, but few are handed the baton when it comes to feeding the bottom line.

If you haven't guessed it already, I am a passionate thought leader and fempreneur when it comes to the healthy disruption of stagnant thinking. As a progressive CEO, I am inspired to support women like me. Women who have raised a family, juggled a household, commanded a boardroom and increased profitability for companies around the world.

And when it comes to business, we need to get clear (and honest) on how the cogs to change fundamentally work. Hiring really does come from the top. We know that HR companies and recruitment executives tap into a pool of regular candidates. This, in turn, ignores any untapped talent resources and reduces the concept of 'fresh blood' into senior roles. At the forefront of my forever-moving mindset is one question, *How can we inspire, lead and achieve gender parity without resistance?*

Behind my purpose is to ensure that any woman can land a high salary if nurtured in the right environment. You see, business needs women. Not just to lessen the gender parity on the current record, which remains fiercely unbalanced, but because we make profits. It doesn't get simpler than that. Inviting a woman onto an executive board cannot be a token gesture. Talking theoretically about diversity, inclusion, equity and equality is no longer enough for corporate giants as they design and implement next-level operational plans. Teasing out the parts of women's leadership is owning the parts of ourselves we were previously asked to mute.

Ladies, get a leg-up, but not a handout. Feel the value of your worth, and if a man is the one to help you, thank him. Difference is everything, but division is dangerous.

Create a team

I am a leader who wears my heart on my sleeve. I am professional, educated, well-travelled and experienced, however, the saying 'putting my work hat on' doesn't ring true with me.

I am transparent and open to forever learning. I understand that true, authentic and inspiring leadership comes with humility.

For me, as someone who has spent thirty-plus years heading up C-suite roles, I know what works and what doesn't.

I have chosen to not be defined by power or wealth.

Don't get me wrong, whilst I am humble, I am also ambitious. However, power and wealth are by-products of good leadership and not solo incentives. Whilst business skills across measurable outcomes are necessary for any leader, whilst impressive on paper, are a little lacking in spirit.

When I was climbing the career ladder, I came across my fair share of scary and also super-approachable leaders. It's almost an old-school management technique to instil fear and remove fairness. As a side effect and symptom of fear before fair, these typical types of leaders can destroy culture and morale, and eventually the bottom line.

So, how do you thrive in leadership?

I want those who work for me to feel like they are working *with* me. I want people to feel valued, heard and encouraged. When we encourage innovation, we uncover ideas, and business always needs new ideas.

For me, honesty is everything.

People will not follow leaders they do not trust. The backbone to any trusted leader is someone who evokes integrity and encourages their teams to be empowered and confident in the work they do.

So how do you create a team culture and still lead from the front?

Be a great decision-maker

Decisive leaders nail strategic direction and are prepared to foot the risks. Don't put your handbrake on at critical moments, because it's in these moments that growth happens.

Be a team player
Foster relationships with your staff and enhance culture with your teams. Don't walk into your office, close the door and segregate yourself from the engine room, but step into the engine room and turn the cogs of the business with those who are backing you!

Be a clear communicator
Don't assume that your direction is a given, but elaborate and seek clarity that your ideas are understood. Listen acutely to your feedback and remove rigidity surrounding your ego!

Great leaders follow as well as lead and become team players, and step up to the leadership podium when required. Robust leaders take responsibility, impart authority and accountability at every turn.

Of course, inspiring leaders are visionaries, inventors, dreamers and disruptors. We need to think into the future and make decisions in the present. By harnessing optimism and a good sense of humour, work is not work, but a place where people will thrive daily.

Building a global network
Let's face it: the world is a much smaller place. Who would have thought that ten years ago – five, even – we would be holding global summits online? The power of connection is fast becoming a prerequisite when it comes to business and networking. [4]Despite the gross economic fallout following the

---

4) wun.ac.uk/wun/research/view/global-research-network-on-the-economic-empowerment-of-women-renew

global pandemic, we are in touch and in tune with one another more than ever. According to a research initiative by Worldwide University Networks (WUN), there is a hypothesis that 'recognising the social, economic and health costs of gender inequality, numerous governments and other global organisations have made women's economic empowerment a key priority'. This would further substantiate the importance of creating a global network with heavy emphasis on women in leadership roles carving a future for economic development.

There are, of course, many types of partnerships, and having the savviness to identify a potential collaboration is key. Networking is more than the exchange of business cards and LinkedIn reviews – it's about tackling issues that matter. From problem-solving coalitions that set out to tackle a particular challenge, to market-shaping investments with multiple stakeholders to address a shortfall in a broken system, we as leaders are now responsible for carving out a virtual process that works.

Success isn't success without sharing the insider hacks that unify a shared goal, so here are some tips to help you level up in the year ahead:

Identify who's who

A key to punching above your weight is to be proactive in exploring collaborative opportunities with leaders, change agents and innovators who share values and goals that are aligned with yours. Your position in the market will have its own strengths, weaknesses, opportunities and threats, so make sure you invest in complementary alliances that build your respective profiles.

Build your community

Personal and professional growth requires regular periods of being stretched and pruned, so if a leader feels like the weakest link, they are positioned exactly where they need to be. Therefore, the value of aligning with those who 'already do' compared to those who 'want to do' is immense. More than ever, authenticity is at the core of a trusted network, so do your research and look for evidence of the narrative you are provided. Real gems sparkle consistently and in all environments.

Identify to innovate

Those at the top of their game spend significant time, money and energy to find innovative ways to stay ahead of the curve. If you, your product and service are not agile, flexible, adaptive and ready to pivot, you may as well pick up your bat and go home. Consumers do not care if your service or product was the 'best' yesterday, they seek a future-focused solution that meets their immediate needs. If you want raving fans, give them what they want and thank them for the opportunity to serve them. Business is all about being the best solution to a problem, so nailing product-to-market fit is critical to your success.

Align with tomorrow's leaders

Prosperity requires planning. Create a network of people who think into the future and explore emerging trends that forecast change in the sector you are working within.

Be obsessed with vision

Your vision must be big, bold and crystal clear. It is the realisation of your dream in all its glory, so be sure it makes your heart sing. Disney's 'to make people happy' or Instagram's 'capture and share the world's moments' are great examples. Mine is 'to help women achieve success, balance and happiness'.

The process can be daunting, but once you get it right and it encapsulates your core ideals, it will provide a road map to where you want to go.

Brainstorm like crazy

The value of taking time out to think creatively is immense. It is in the quiet that you can bounce ideas around and let them run their course without interruption and the impact of society's magnet. Innovative thinking requires an acceptance that all ideas have the right to be explored. Imagining what the seemingly impossible looks like is a great place to start. Remember, Steve Jobs dreamt of finding a way to put your favourite songs in your pocket! Always have a journal nearby to capture your ideas and make sure you include the somewhat-left-field ones as they may not be as crazy as you think.

Collective action

To lead change and disrupt the norm, working across multiple sectors, platforms and time zones is key. It will allow you more opportunity to create a synergic force that builds its own momentum and strengthens its resolve. You need to adapt and pivot when navigating a period of unforeseen change, so be prepared to continually expand your network as you enhance the profile of your vision.

Keep up the pace

Creating global partnerships means investing heavily in your community. As a CEO, I know what it's like to juggle a million balls in the air. The key is to never drop the glass ones.

Throughout my career, I have learnt how to apply and win business growth through strategy and designing methods that work. But I would much prefer to emerge from a lockdown with my global partners. Let's learn, educate and inspire one another to kick some ambitious goals.

ANNIE GIBBINS

Starting her career as a registered nurse, Annie went on to become a health educationist, change management CEO and entrepreneur whilst raising her family of five, including two sets of twins born twenty-six months apart.

Annie Gibbins is a passionate and purpose-driven 'fempreneur', global women's empowerment coach, CEO, podcast host, speaker and number-one bestselling author.

Positioned as one of Australia's leading voices for women in leadership and founder of The Women's Business Incubator and The Women's Business Tribe, Annie is a digital powerhouse helping women push the limits of what is truly possible.

As G100 Australia Country Chair – Equity & Equality, her passion for gender equality is unwavering when it comes to excelling the potential of the female workforce. Annie is driven by demolishing the glass ceiling and removing the invisible barriers to success that many women come up against in their business and life journey.

As the host of *Memoirs of Successful Women*, Annie has interviewed hundreds of inspirational women worldwide. Her continuous portfolio of high-calibre podcast guests range from business leaders, entrepreneurs, humanitarians, athletes and the creators of startups on a mission.

With three university degrees under her belt and twenty years of executive change management experience, Annie is now a go-to inspirational global speaker. In 2020, she earned the distinguished 'Unsung Business Hero' title in recognition of her formidable courage, compassion, perseverance, conviction and selflessness when coaching women to thrive. Speaking at the World Economic Forum, Annie shared the importance of engagement with political, business and cultural leaders to shape global, regional and industry agendas.

As a keynote speaker at the 'Lady America Power: Barriers and Bias, The Status of Women in Leadership' in 2021, Annie shared the power behind unlocking the visibility of female entrepreneurs around the globe. This prestigious event celebrated women internationally, heralding the importance of women in leadership.

Global brand, Hoinser Group, dedicated to promoting outstanding individuals in business throughout Europe, Africa, Asia, UAE and USA, invited Annie to their collective as an honourable member, elevating her influence tenfold.

Annie has graced covers and written articles for books and magazines including *1 Habit Leadership, I am Woman Global, Lady Speaker Power, Success, Hoinser, W, CIO Times,* and *MO2VATE Magazine*. She was named Top Women's Change Maker and Global Goodwill Ambassador in 2021.

DELIVERING EXEMPLARY CUSTOMER SERVICE

Angela Schutz

Customer service is often the unsung hero of an organisation. When an organisation understands the importance of putting a conscientious effort into training its employees in delivering exemplary customer service, they will ultimately achieve customer loyalty and reap the profits they desire. The organisation that embraces the concept of having employees on every level be attentive to the needs of the customer will create an environment that is attractive to the customer.

Have you ever gone into a business and felt completely invisible because no-one even looked up to ask if you needed help? How did it make you feel? Did you think, *I want to come here again,* or did you feel you should walk out and never come back? When you think about it, you may even conclude that you could spend your money elsewhere.

Often, people go to organisations that offer inferior products simply because they were treated as if they were VIP customers. The staff were well-informed and courteous and perhaps they even remembered the customer's name. The products may not have been especially great, but the atmosphere was extremely inviting.

The organisation that remembers the names and other details of a customer will build a strong relationship with that customer. They feel special and want to come back repeatedly. They freely recommend that business to others simply because they were made to feel special.

Customer service is the personal responsibility of every member of an organisation, and it is the one area that distinguishes you from your competitors.

How do you achieve that level of customer service within your organisation? Whether you are a solopreneur or the owner of a large corporation, you can create an atmosphere that will attract and keep good customers.

Organisational change always comes from the top down in order for it to last. Do you, as the leader, practice good customer service with everyone you meet? How do you respond to your family and friends? How do you treat your staff and customers?

In my coaching business, it's a priority that the bond between my clients and myself is one of strength. It is important to build good rapport with the client in order to establish a trusting relationship. Clients are my livelihood, after all. Over the years, I have developed some exceptional customer service practices that I have used to keep my clients coming back for coaching.

Here are some basic concepts that are the cornerstones of customer service I stand by:

1. Treat everyone with the utmost respect. Know that everyone is a VIP to someone; make them feel as if they are a VIP

to you. It all starts with the simple act of remembering the person's name. If they tell you personal information about themselves, remember it. If they tell you about their family structure or their pets, remember the details and inquire about those who are precious to your client. It makes them respect you more. If you have a difficult time remembering so many details, keep a file on each customer to which you can refer before interacting with them.

2. There is always an emotional element in customer service. Find the person's pain point or tender spot, and you will do well. Remember, they have come to you because they need something, and whether it be a product or a service, they feel you are the best one to provide that for them. It will benefit you if you explore why they need your product or service. With that knowledge, you can point out the selling points of working with you. It will solidify both the relationship and their loyalty. It will also help them get clarity about their needs and goals. It makes working with them so much easier.

3. Look them in the eye! I used to work in a home for developmentally challenged adults. Whenever they had to talk to me, they would look down. I would often ask them if they owed me money. That would cause them to look at me and say: 'No!' 'Then, look me in the eye,' I would say. There is power in eye contact. It is the first step in creating a relationship.

4. Be authentic. People sense when your words and actions aren't in alignment. Say what you mean and mean what you say. When you make a time commitment to deliver service at a specific time, be sure to arrive on time. If you are running late, renegotiate the time commitment rather than just arriving late … or not at all. One trick I use is to agree on the time

of our next appointment and then I ask my client to call me at that time. It keeps you from ever being late. If they call you late, it cuts into their appointment, but they take the responsibility of the lateness, not you.

5. If you deliver a service that requires you to enter someone's home or office, clean up after yourself. Leave the space the way you found it ... or better. Be mindful that the homeowner or business owner expects that you will treat their things with utmost respect.

6. Communication is key! Always listen more than talk. The more you allow a client to talk about themselves, the more they like you! Some people take a while to open up, so if you are always trying to make a point, you may be cutting off communication. Listen carefully, because when people have the opportunity to be freely expressive, they often reveal more than they would normally. Remember to never repeat any private information you hear. Protect the client's privacy.

7. Non-verbal communication is just, if not more, important than verbal communication. If you don't seem happy to be with your client, or you roll your eyes at what they are saying, they will get the message loud and clear that you don't really care about them. If you have employees that sit at the first desk a client sees, be sure that they greet each client in an upbeat manner, make eye contact and are ready to address the needs of the client.

'I don't know' is never an answer a client should hear. The frontline employee should always be ready to spring into action to find an answer to the needs of the customers. That can only happen if the manager has taken the time to train that person.

8. When it comes to rules, the Golden Rule is always best, but I like to put a twist on it. Do unto others better than they would do unto you. Instead of using the 'what's in it for me' (WIIFM) approach, use the 'how can I serve' (HCIS) approach. What do you bring to the table that your clients love? What keeps them coming back? If you don't know, ask them. I like to use a simple evaluation form that gives me the kind of feedback I need to assess how I am doing.

   Simply say: 'On a scale from one to ten, how happy were you with my service this week?' If it isn't a ten, ask, 'What would have made it a ten for you?'

   When you think of how you can best serve your client, there may be a time when your client needs a referral or a LinkedIn recommendation, so give them one, and while you are at it, ask them for a recommendation on LinkedIn for yourself and your business in return.

   In this day and age, clients are very savvy. They read reviews before making any purchase. The more positive reviews about you and your business, the faster your business will grow.

9. Have a call to action for your clients. Human beings love to get something for nothing or something at a reduced price. Offer your service at a reduced rate if they bring in a new paying customer for you or offer them a discount fee if they sign up for your service by midnight.

10. Let technology work for you. There are so many high-tech programs that enable you to keep track of details like a client's birthday or other memorable occasions. Set up reminders so that you can send out e-cards for their birthday, etc. And speaking of birthdays, make a special offer to your clients on YOUR birthday. You can offer them a reduced rate in your services, or you can donate to a great cause

and ask them to do the same. Invite them to do good in the world with you!
11. A great deal of customer service principles use some of the same principles as those used in marketing. There are many promotional products on which you can put the name of your business. Find inexpensive items that can be engraved with the name of your business.

    I love to write books. I have had bookmarks created to give as gifts to those who buy the book. I also wrote a book titled *A Boomer Chick's Guide to Online Dating – You're Never Too Old to Look and Love*. I wrote it during the pandemic when so many of us were getting vaccinated. When I thought about a small gift to give away at book signings, I came up with the idea to have a vaccine card holder made that was clear on one side and red on the other. It said *Boomer Chick* and gave my website address. People love gifts and they are carrying around your website or email information that many others can see.

Motivating your staff to always deliver quality customer service

If your goal is to treat your customers in a way that they feel so special that they want to be loyal to you, you need to employ some basic tactics that will keep your staff motivated to deliver quality service all the time. Here are some tips that will keep your staff motivated.

Value

Your staff love getting paid for an honest day's work, but coupling that pay cheque with a sense that their work is of value to the organisation is the secret sauce for keeping your staff working at the highest level. Noticing when a staff member goes over and above when dealing with a customer will go a long way to keep them motivated.

Having a voice
Giving your staff a chance to make suggestions, and whenever possible, putting into practice those things that make sense for your organisation will make your staff members feel valued.

Open communication
There are times when problems pop up. Don't hide things from your staff. When they worry that there is something that will shake the stability of the organisation – or worse, their job security – talk with them so that they don't jump to the worst possible conclusion.

Flexibility
Very often you will have individuals on staff who have hidden talents. They can envision things that no-one else has thought of. Give them the opportunity to grow by giving them some extra power to make decisions on how to do things. Don't make them always ask for permission to get things done. That flexibility will add to the efficiency of the organisation.

You can also install suggestion boxes that will allow employees to make suggestions and remain anonymous if they like. Let them see those suggestions put into action or mention the suggestions at a staff meeting.

Go the distance
There is nothing better than a surprise! When you 'catch' a staff member going the distance for a customer, give them a reward. It can be small, but just to be recognised for doing a good job

makes a huge difference to the employee. This can be done on an individual basis, or you can reward the entire staff by taking them to lunch, having a social event for them or even bringing in a masseuse to do chair massages in a private room.

Show me the money

Of course, a bonus or any extra monetary 'thank you' is always motivating, but surprisingly, employees actually respond extremely well to other forms of approval. Having an 'employee of the month' program that recognises a staff member in each department every month is a fun way to motivate the staff and keep the morale up. You can give the monthly winner an Amazon (or other) gift card.

The power of the pen

Years ago, I worked in an organisation where I had two administrative assistants. My job kept me very busy. There were days when I had six meetings to attend in a day. I hardly saw my admins. I started to hear some of my colleagues talk about how lucky I was to have such an efficient and gregarious staff. They often saw the admins helping other staff members and visitors.

I knew my workload would not change, but I wanted to let my admins know how much I appreciated them. Every Thursday before I left work I sat down and wrote them each a thank you note. On Friday morning when they got to work, they were greeted with a note on their desks. It wasn't long before I heard amazing stories from others about how fabulous my staff were.

These women wanted to please me because I showed them how much I appreciated them. A simple thank you note can bring about major positive changes in an organisation.

What are the financial impacts of delivering exemplary customer service?

It is so easy to assume that customer service is simply about the way we treat our customers and staff, but there is a tremendous financial gain to delivering exemplary service. Every business needs to keep a funnel full of customers all the time. What we need from those customers is both loyalty and the profits they bring us through their purchases and the referrals they send our way. When we do the research on how much we gain financially from keeping good customers, we are surprised at the outcomes.

Let's take some time to look at the facts:

Customer retention is the key to success, especially for small businesses. Approximately 50% of annual revenue is from repeat customers (BIA and Kelsey). Remember, repeat purchases are not accidental! If your customers like you and your product or service, they will come back over and over, and the result will be higher profits, a better reputation and a greater footprint in the industry.

Repeat customers refer to 50% more potential buyers than one-time buyers (Bain and Co) and 92% of shoppers trust word-of-mouth recommendations over other forms of marketing (Nielsen).

Many years ago there was a commercial on TV that brought about a good point. It said that if a customer liked your product, they would tell two friends, who would tell two friends, who would tell two friends, and so on and so on! Word of mouth is powerful! It can make or break the reputation of a company. Today we have social media such as Facebook, Instagram, Tik-Tok and Yelp that each serve as a strong network that has that very same power.

A whopping 80% of future profits come from 20% of your current customers (Gartner; Martech).

It costs sixteen times more to bring a new customer up to the same level of spending as a current customer. It is worth all your effort to keep your current customers.

Long-term positives of exemplary customer service

Having a reputation for giving exemplary customer service can increase your reputation in the industry and help you increase your footprint. You always want to be the company that comes to mind when someone is looking for a particular product or service. You want to be the most highly recommended company in your industry. That can and will happen consistently if you always go the extra mile for your customers.

If you own a small business or are a solo entrepreneur, it stands to reason that there are many ways in which you cannot compete with larger organisations. One way is that you don't have the buying power to buy in such quantities as to get a lower price on orders. You must sell at a higher cost, and of course, that brings about the thought that customers won't buy from you because, comparatively, your items are priced higher than the larger organisations.

It is interesting that customers would rather pay a higher price and give their business to a smaller organisation that delivers quality customer service rather than go with the less expensive item from a company that doesn't care about them. All of your efforts to be at the top in the delivery of customer service will defray any negativity associated with selling at a higher price.

Good customer care gives you a competitive advantage. In a time where customers often complain about the lack of service or the feeling that they mean little to a business, providing excellent customer service can set you apart from your competitors.

It's true that customers want the best product for the best price, but if you can produce the best product and back it up with quality customer service, you will outshine and outsell all your competitors.

Consistency is key. How can you be assured that you can deliver quality customer service? Train your staff well and monitor the delivery of service. Have you ever been to a restaurant where the food was sublime, but the service was horrible? You dream about the food, but every time you think about the way you were treated, you vow never to go back. The reason that happens is that the manager is not overseeing the quality of the service. Imagine having to close a culinarily superb restaurant because the service was subpar? It should never happen!

We've discussed the importance of training your staff so that there is a cohesive group of employees delivering quality service in the same way. There is another benefit to putting in the effort to have a united front when delivering customer service and that's to your employees themselves. When an employee works for an organisation that has high ethical standards and always treats the staff and customers with respect, they develop a sense of pride in their work and a true loyalty to the organisation. They develop a true appreciation for the values upon which you run your organisation, and as the organisation's reputation goes up in the community, the employees' esteem of the owners of the organisation goes up as well.

Your employees will take pride in working for you and they will continue to serve your customers well.

There are red flags all over when an organisation has poor retention of staff. Just as having loyal customers increases your profits, so does retention of staff. It costs you money to have to train new employees. Whether you personally do the training or have another staff member do it, you are spending company dollars for training rather than for selling to customers.

In conclusion, create a plan to develop strong customer service policies that will foster the satisfaction of both your staff and your customers.

As a consequence of putting solid practices into place, your business will thrive and grow with the loyalty and profits you desire.

[1]*Statistics sourced from Bain & Co, Nielsen and Constant Contact.*

---

1) bain.com

ANGELA SCHUTZ

Angela Schutz is the founder of Driven to Succeed Consulting, LLC – a career coaching and professional development company.

She has helped hundreds land new, meaningful jobs, dispelling the myth that there are no jobs out there! Put simply, Angela helps the unemployed go from hopeless to happily employed. Angela taught human resources management for eleven years and has led a woman's group called Dream Dare Dance, moving women to create new dreams, daring themselves to move forward and celebrate their victories!

Angela's passion is for writing! In 2012 she published her first book: *Career Questions? Ask Angela – A Job-Seeker's Guide to Finding the Perfect Job*. Since 2012, she has co-authored twelve community books on gratitude and co-authored *A Woman's*

Journey – Stories of Substance, Survival and Success and *The Book on Joy*.

In 2021 Angela wrote *A Boomer Chick's Guide to Online Dating – You're Never Too Old to Look and Love*. In 2021, she was interviewed by Star Jones and was inducted into *Who's Who in America*. In 2022 she was inducted into *Who's Who in Professional Women*. She was a keynote speaker in the Herrington Publications Worldwide conference: Lady Politico Power Global Leadership Conference.

Angela remains humbled and honoured by these awards.

BREAKING THROUGH IMPOSTER SYNDROME

Annette Densham

Who do you think you are?

Inside most of us there is a little voice who is the bane of our existence. This little voice sounds like us. Instead of encouraging us to shine and be the best we can be, it spews doubt and fear into our hearts and heads, stopping us from taking even the smallest step.

That little voice, otherwise known as the 'itty bitty shitty committee', is poison to personal progress, as it puts up walls and barriers. Think about it. The last time you did something outside your comfort zone, what was that inner voice telling you?

Chances are, if it is anything like mine, it said …
Who do you think you are?
You can't do that; you are too dumb.
You haven't done enough to enter an award.

People will find out you are a fraud.
You are not worth it.
Or is that just me?

I know it is not just me. The 'Impostor Phenomenon' paper written by Jaruwan Sakulku and James Alexander and featured in *The International Journal of Behavioural Science,* found 70% of high achievers suffer from this pesky thing called imposter syndrome. Imposter syndrome is the belief you are not as competent as others perceive you to be. It is an insidious curse that stifles creativity, innovation and performance ... and we do it to ourselves.

You are not alone

Talk about gluttons for punishment. It may make you feel a little better to know it is not just you. You are in great company.

Tom Hanks is a certifiable movie star. For over forty-five years, he has been entertaining us with iconic characters like Forrest Gump, Woody, Walt Disney and Jim Lovel. He's won two Oscars, eighty-nine other awards and over two hundred nominations. He's successful. Would it surprise you that imposter syndrome racks him?

In an interview with a [1]magazine in 2016 for *A Hologram for the King,* he shared that he still doubts his acting abilities. He said, 'No matter what we've done, there comes a point where you think, *How did I get here? When will they discover that I am a fraud and take everything away from me?*'

What about the highly talented Lady Gaga? She has won thirteen Grammys and an Academy Award, two Golden Globe Awards, sixteen Guinness World Records and the inaugural

---

[1] npr.org/2016/04/26/475573489/tom-hanks-says-self-doubt-is-a-high-wire-act-that-we-all-walk?t=1659503395170

Songwriters Hall of Fame's Contemporary Icon Award. It is safe to say she is a genius in her space. But in her HBO special, she said, 'I still sometimes feel like a loser kid in high school, and I just have to pick myself up and tell myself that I'm a superstar every morning, so that I can get through this day and be what my fans want me to be.'

My favourite artist is David Bowie. He may be gone, but he definitely is not forgotten. The mark he left on music and fashion ripples through society today. Not only was he a successful music artist selling over one hundred million records globally, he's had a spider and an asteroid named after him, transitioned from music to the silver screen, and starred in hit movies like *Labyrinth* and *Merry Christmas Mr. Lawrence*. He hid his self-doubt behind work. He said, 'I had enormous self-image problems and very low self-esteem, which I hid behind obsessive writing and performing … I was driven to get through life quickly. I felt so utterly inadequate. I thought the work was the only thing of value.'

Then there is me.

I grew up in a time where children were seen and not heard. I was regularly told as a child not to 'show off', 'big note' myself or to talk about myself – it was deemed impolite and self-absorbed. When I started in business, I left the relative safety of corporate life where I could hide behind my role in my cubicle and not have to be in the spotlight. But going into business changes all that, because if you are not promoting what you do and sharing your stories, you fade into the background, leaving the space to be dominated by those who use their voice.

In business, there is no room for modesty; there is nowhere to hide if you want to make your mark. The heart of business growth is marketing and how you tell your stories. That pesky imposter syndrome gets in the way.

When I started my business, I had to learn how to overcome self-doubt to put myself out there; who starts a business to be the best-kept secret? No-one! It took me many years to get comfortable with being unconformable in the spotlight. I have gone from never ever speaking about what I do to dominating social media and Myspace, because I realised that if it was to be, it was up to me.

No-one else was going to promote my business for me. I had to do it. I had to learn how to overcome self-doubt. People now tell me how inspirational I am, how brave I am, how bold I am and how confident I am, because it seems like I am everywhere. I still have moments of crippling self-doubt, but I know that I have to keep showing up.

You do not need a phone box to find your superpower

If movers and shakers like these three (and me) struggle with self-doubt and questioning who they are, what hope do you have? How do you turn that nagging, negative voice of self-doubt into a superpower?

Self-doubt can be a superpower. Okay, self-doubt is never fun, but a certain amount is healthy. Healthy self-doubt means you are reflective and responsible with your actions. It separates us from narcissists. But if you change how you view self-doubt from a crippling kryptonite to an empowering rocket ship, then you will unblock your ability to get shit done. Because it is you that is stopping your growth.

You can use it to move through doubt into a place of personal empowerment and audacious action. Self-doubt as a superpower looks like objective when it comes to the work you do – you do not just charge into the unknown without looking at the next steps from all angles. Self-doubt as a superpower means you are open to asking for help. Self-doubt as a superpower gives you space to evaluate what you do and why you do it. Self-doubt as a superpower leads to greater self-awareness and reflection. Self-doubt as a superpower protects you from what is called the Dunning-Kruger effect – people who overestimate their abilities and knowledge, especially in a space they have no experience in. You know the types; TV talent shows are full of them.

What type of imposter are you?

Self-doubt is healthy. But where it strays into unhealthy is when it consumes you, and imposter syndrome becomes your travelling companion.

As with most problems in life, the best way to surmount them is to take responsibility and acknowledge it is a problem.

As you begin the journey to overcoming imposter syndrome, it is good to name the type of imposter syndrome you suffer from. Chances are you are a perfectionist or someone who is used to getting things done without help, or naturally talented and skilled in your space. There are four types of imposters:

- Perfectionist.
- Superhero.
- Good at everything.
- Party of one.

Which one are you?

Perfectionist (I have more to say later in the chapter)

Perfectionism and imposter syndrome go hand-in-hand. Do you relate to these traits?

- Set excessively high goals.
- Everything has to be 100% perfect all the time.
- When you fail to reach a goal, you spiral into self-doubt and anxiety.
- Have to be in absolute control of everything.
- The only person who can do it right is you.
- Focus only on results.
- Crippling fear of failure.
- Defensiveness if a mistake is pointed out.
- Highly critical.
- Find it impossible to delegate, and if you do, you have to change everything to suit your ideals.
- Procrastinate if things do not fall perfectly into place.

Superhero

Otherwise known as martyrs or workaholics. The superheroes are the ones who cover up their insecurities by being the first to put up their hand for a new project, setting out to prove their value. The superhero must be good at everything, through all areas of their life. Do you relate to these traits?

- First in and last to leave.
- Business or work is your primary focus.
- Doubt yourself even though you are highly educated and trained.
- Downtime stresses you out because you should be working.
- Hate being criticised.

- Find it impossible to feel good about yourself even when you get a pat on the back.

Good at everything
This imposter syndrome type feels they have to be naturally good at everything. If it takes too long to learn something, they have failed. Do you relate to these traits?

- Set the bar ridiculously high.
- Have to get things right the first time.
- If you do not pick something up, you beat yourself up.
- Your self-talk includes, *Why am I so stupid?* or, *I'm a loser for not getting that right.*
- You excel without putting in too much effort – things come easily for you.
- A straight A student.
- Won lots of awards.
- Shy away from coaching or mentoring – you don't need it.
- You're the 'smart one' in the family.
- Avoid challenges because you do not want to fail.

Party of one
A close cousin is good at everything, and an aspect of imposter syndrome sufferers, do not like asking for help. Asking for help is a sign of weakness and lack of knowledge and skill. A highly independent type, party of one never asks for help. Do you relate to these traits?

- Don't need anyone else's input to finish a job.
- You are the expert.
- You're always upskilling, so you never need anyone else's help.

- You feel like you don't know enough.
- You take on all the responsibility.
- You prefer to work alone.
- If people offer to help you, you politely decline.

The FRAUD factor

There are five steps on the pathway to donning your superpower cape and turning down the volume on the negative Nancy in your head.

- Fess up – talk about how you feel.
- Reality – acknowledge what is real and what you are making up in your head.
- Acceptance – change how you view failure and mistakes.
- Undergo – do you want a growth or fixed mindset?
- Delight – start celebrating your wins.

Fess up, people

Once you know this, you can overcome feeling like a fraud by fessing up.

The problem with being human is that we think that if we speak our foibles and weaknesses out loud, we'll be judged. Maybe by some, but vulnerability and speaking honestly about the human condition will take these taboo and stigmatised topics into the mainstream, making it more comfortable for others to recover from imposter syndrome. Never be afraid to talk about the challenges you face in life. You will probably help more people than you realise by being honest and open.

Reality check

The next step is to work out if that 'itty bitty shitty committee' is a voice of truth or an evil voice intent on sabotaging your life. The problem with that voice inside our head is it doesn't know the difference between fact and fiction. Your brain believes what you tell it. If you always tell yourself that you suck, then that's exactly the space you come from. But if you tell yourself you are awesome, you start to believe it. Affirmations are a powerful tool to change your internal program. Even though it feels weird standing in front of a mirror telling yourself how good you are, just do it. Before long, you start to see yourself differently. It just takes practice.

It is okay to not be perfect

One of the smartest men on the planet, the late Stehen Hawking, said, when asked about the formation of the universe, 'One of the basic rules of the universe is that nothing is perfect. Perfection simply doesn't exist … Without imperfection, neither you nor I would exist.'

Somewhere on our life journey, the message has come through loud and clear that perfectionism is a character strength, but all I see from people who aim for perfection is stress, anxiety and a fixation on control, all of which twists and contorts them into an all-or-nothing approach to life. Perfectionists have an overwhelming fear of failure, and mistakes can send them into a festering whirlpool of procrastination and hyper-criticalness of self. There are studies to show perfectionists achieve way less than us regular high achievers. It is hard to let go of perfectionism, but if you can and are willing to embrace failure and mistakes, you will learn so much more. Making mistakes and failing makes us humans more resilient, gives us opportunities to learn and grow and makes us way more interesting to others.

Your brain is plastic, you can change
After you have sorted out what is real in your head, you can then move onto growth. Years ago, Dr Carol Dweck wrote *Mindset: The New Psychology of Success*, where she explored the difference between a fixed and growth mindset. Those who struggle to move forward are stuck in a fixed mindset; a little like cement of the grey matter, getting stuck in the details and the way things have always been done. Your abilities are not carved in stone, and failing is an opportunity to learn and grow – this is underpinned by a growth mindset. If you can start to acknowledge that your talents and abilities can be developed, learning something new is good and is how you get smarter and more resilient, that little voice tends to shush. There is no final destination for those who invest in personal development. Growing, learning and changing are all important elements of being human. We are works in progress.

Celebrate your wins … all of them
Finally, take delight in the everyday and know that it is okay to celebrate your wins and mourn your losses and that life is not perfect. Hey, if Stephen Hawking, one of the smartest men on the planet, tells you the universe is not perfect, then why do you expect to be?

Give yourself a daily boost
While I am not a big fan of faking it until you make it, sometimes we need a few hacks to trick us on our journey to turning self-doubt into a superpower. When that voice is nagging you, strike a pose – a power pose. Amy Cuddy's TED Talk on power posing shared that an expansive body posture, like Superman's, can uplift your mood and attitude. Stand like a superhero, hands on hips,

chin up, chest out for five minutes, and tell me that doesn't make you feel more powerful.

We are all human, trying to do our best and get ahead. It is time to stop giving ourselves a hard time. You deserve to live a wonderful life; stop getting in your own way.

ANNETTE DENSHAM

Annette Densham is an award-winning PR and business awards specialist, which sometimes still surprises her because the only award she'd ever won was the Top Dog Achievement Award in grade two. Losing her cushy corporate comms role, she had to reinvent herself, stepping out from behind the keyboard to build her own PR agency.

Using her print journalism and corporate communications skills, she works with entrepreneurs and businesses to build Googlicious profiles by sharing their stories across multiple channels, winning them awards and getting them featured in the media.

WHY SEGMENTING YOUR MARKET SMALLER MAKES FOR BIGGER BUSINESS

Ayumi Uyeda

Discovery overseas

'You've sold five boxes, you need to drop the price,' is what my boss (the head of Asia-Pacific) said in a group conference call only three months after we launched. I was furious. And as our marketing director and I glanced at each other, we let it go. In that one glance, we understood each other well.

We had come so far and were 100% aligned on our strategy, and we had full belief in our teams and our plans, and we would not entertain a price drop for volume. We needed to do better to buy more time and show quick wins that the strategy was working.

We had just started up operations to enter the market for a large multinational in Japan – a market that is notorious for failing multinationals – and as this was the third attempt for the company, the long memories of the market were not forgiving of our past nor welcoming of our arrival.

And after completing the research and development of a pregnancy supplement to prevent birth defects, designed and formulated for Japanese women, taking into account their specific dietary needs, deficiencies and behaviours, we knew we had a product that would change the trajectory of increasing birth defects that Japan had seen since the 1970s.

Our product was more expensive than most supplements that were sold in drugstores, and we had made a conscious decision to not distribute through mass channels but to distribute directly via obstetricians and gynaecologists, who could provide the education needed to change the course.

We were committed to working with specialists and the government to reverse the climbing birth defects, and to do this, significant education was required. We were there to shine a light on the hair-raising upwards-trending graph that was not seen in any other market around the world.

For a country that had incredibly high health care accessibility, safety standards and care for its citizens, this was not a situation that was readily accepted, let alone addressed. So, dropping the price and selling mass was not the answer to overcoming what we saw as a major public health issue. It would take time and a lot of effort and endurance.

This situation was not an uncommon one, and throughout my career, I have been met many times with instruction to expand, extend or mimic competition all in the name of securing higher volumes of short-term sales. There is always the temptation to secure 'easy sales' which might be okay if a cheap-and-cheery generic volume-based business is the strategy. But if you're in the business of building brands and solving real problems that are yet to be solved, it requires focus, consistency and time.

Driving change is a long road but is, without doubt, one of the most exciting and rewarding roads travelled. And in this case, we needed to start with a very specific group of mums-to-be. We had learned that for women planning pregnancy, the most receptive to education were women who were older, who may have found that falling pregnant didn't happen so easily and were willing to do everything possible for a healthy baby. So, from there, we started with a small but highly motivated segment of women.

The word 'segment' is one I first heard in Mexico. Although I had trained as a pharmacist in Brisbane, Australia, and spent most of my time as a pharmacist in the clinical setting in hospitals, there was a time when I found myself unemployed, knocking on doors looking for work.

This might sound odd, as at that time in the late 1990s, pharmacists were in high demand, and with the shortage of pharmacists, it was known to be one of the most economically protected professions in Australia. And while that was true, I had taken a different path – one that all my friends, family and colleagues tried to talk me out of and in fact made me feel like I was making a detrimental mistake in my life and career. 'The world is your oyster,' they would tell me at the age of twenty-two, 'Why would you leave your hospital job?'

I was restless.

I was always restless and in a hurry. I was always looking for ways to speed up things, speed up my postgrad degree, speed up the experience I could get so I could get a job faster and race the clock, because every minute lost was a minute I would never get back.

I had had a dream since I was fourteen to work for a

pharmaceutical company, 'invent' life-changing drugs and keep going. I had taken the chance to travel around South America with my sister for two months, and as we were finishing up our travels in Mexico, it was time for me to head back to my hospital job in Brisbane. After immersing myself in a cultural smorgasbord, I couldn't let it go. I saw the end of this trip as the end of a great adventure, and I wasn't ready for it to end.

I decided it would not be the end, but it would be the beginning of a whole new adventure. At the time, many pharmaceutical companies in Mexico battled it out with Argentina for regional headquarters in Latin America. And as it had been my goal to work in pharmaceuticals, I thought it would be an ideal chance to apply for jobs with the pharmaceutical companies I had read so much about. On my list were the likes of Pharmacia, Novartis, Merck and Janssen. The jobs I applied for were mainly sales representative positions, and the ads typically had specific criteria:

- Must be male thirty to thirty-five years.
- Must be married.
- Must have own car.

Perhaps unsurprisingly, I was unsuccessful in finding work, and after interviewing with a good twenty to thirty pharmaceutical companies, the 30% unemployment level at the time, my lack of a working visa and my lack of Spanish, I found myself to be unemployable. Oh, and I was twenty-two and looked about fourteen (yes, people would still ask me what I wanted to be when I grew up), but yet some companies had me back for three or four interviews, which still resulted in the same outcome.

It was a drastic change from the 'economically protected' profession of a pharmacist back home. As good fortune would have it,

I did eventually land a position at an advertising agency; and little did I know, it was a top-three agency at the time and headquartered in New York City. It was just lucky that the general manager who interviewed me (and I still don't know why a GM was doing the first-round interview), saw that I was Australian and said, 'Right, we'll do the interview in English then!' He proceeded to hire me on the spot without even testing out my Spanish.

The New York office soon learned that I might also be able to help them as they were, at the time, struggling with two of their pharmaceutical clients – Eli Lilly and Company and Janssen – which were focused on recruiting patients for clinical trials. There was a time in the late nineties when the market was full of blockbuster drugs hitting the market, and with the high number of clinical trials underway, the market was saturated and there was a shortage of patients for the trials, so they had started to use advertising tactics to recruit patients.

A big part of the problem was that the protocols for the clinical trials were written with the goal of ensuring data sets were as clean as possible, and the criteria for a patient to be eligible was very tight and ruled out many other medical conditions, medications and lifestyle factors. These criteria were so tight that it became questionable as to whether these specific patients actually existed. And so, I started to offer a viewpoint on the trial protocols and their inclusion and exclusion criteria.

I researched population demographics, contacted advocacy groups for data on specific diseases and medical conditions, asked for population statistics and prevalence rates, and I started to size the market for the criteria of patients in the protocols. I could start to see if there was a gap between the market and the desired inclusion criteria for patients.

From there, I could suggest small changes in inclusion or

exclusion criteria to broaden the pool of potential candidates, while keeping the data 'clean' so that a trial could be completed and the efforts wouldn't be wasted with a 'failed trial' due to 'failed recruitment'. Protocol reviews then became a unique offering for the agency and one which was not offered by any other advertising agency.

This was one form of segmentation in action. The NY office offered me a job to transfer, which I leapt at, and as I was arriving in the dot-com era, it was an exciting, bustling time to be there and offered a chance for a highly compressed learning environment.

In advertising, we educated our clients on the importance of market segmentation, and it was in the US that I learned that not only is the US not one market, but even NY is made up of many market segments. Our advertising was segmented by culture and language for Caucasian, Hispanic and African-American audiences, and we sub-segmented further by education level, family influence characteristics and socioeconomic parameters.

It was here that I learned the importance of tailoring communication to specific consumer segments and its impact, and we tweaked radio scripts and newspaper ads to get the language right for each segment.

While I was fortunate to have had the chance to learn these lessons very early in my career (I was twenty-five by then), it was when I returned to Australia that I saw segmentation was given less importance, perhaps because populations were smaller and less heterogeneous.

And much later in my career, we learned the expensive lessons of not defining specific enough segments to serve when launching products. In Australia, we have had great success with Elevit – a pregnancy supplement – and it seemed like a logical step to offer a 'mums' multi' for new mums between their pregnancies. But despite this strong loyalty to Elevit, this failed after a few years, and it came back to not understanding what mums wanted and needed at that time in their lives.

Focusing on being focused is easier said than done. The voices all around us, the words of wisdom of those who have been there before (or so they claim), the hamster wheel of quarterly demands from shareholders to sell more, build faster, expand quicker and chase the shiny and new are ever-present.

What's nice about running a small country like Singapore or New Zealand in a multinational is that it's not seen as an important country. It's not the USA or Germany or China. And when it's not big and important there are fewer people trying to 'help', less interference and much greater latitude for experimentation.

While these are the markets with tiny budgets, there is immense opportunity for innovation and a 'try-and-see' approach, and because budgets are tiny, choices are forced. They say limitations give birth to innovation, and when we can't afford to run full marketing campaigns or launch a product everywhere, we are forced to make decisive choices on whom we will serve, where we distribute and how we will communicate to our consumers. I cut my teeth stretching out shoestring budgets and honed my skills in navigating complexity in small countries and regions while inside large companies.

Back home

I met a stranger in the street today. We talked for about half an hour, and it all started with a smile as he reached out to pat my dog. So, I stopped. Over the last six years, walking my dog has opened the opportunity for me to stop and talk to many people – not that I'm an extrovert or one to strike up a conversation, but a chat that starts with a dog's age or name can lead you down some very interesting paths. Today I learned that this particular fellow claimed to have written the copy for the award-winning anti-litter campaign in 1979 *Do the right thing.*

This came up towards the end of the conversation, and along the way he shared a number of his anecdotes, interviews with interesting people in the USA (celebrities like Robert Redford and Frank Sinatra), winning the Cannes Festival awards for ads he'd created, things people had told him about his voice, that it was made for flowing across the airways, and how he'd been helping a local independent candidate in their political campaign until he asked them to 'include me out because of the politics'.

Although my post-conversation googling turned up nothing about him, I began to reflect on the idea that while today's youth generation captures their highlight reels on social media, the generations before also have a highlight reel stored within their memories, which for them, are perhaps the truth of what they have lived through.

I grew up observing and knowing what hard work looked like. My parents ran their own tourism business in Brisbane, and they focused on the Japanese tourist market. The fax machine, which they bought in 1984, was game-changing technology for them as they could suddenly communicate in writing with their referring counterparts in Japan.

My father, who is Japanese, managed all the 'allocations' of some two-hundred-plus Japanese tour guides, who were mostly in Australia on working-holiday visas and were responsible for the airport-to-hotel transfers which included tour guiding for the passengers, and he did this with a pencil (a Pacer, and he always had a good supply of lead) and a giant red book which was set up just like a spreadsheet.

My mother, who is Australian, managed all the financial and

operational aspects such as hotel bookings, reservations and balancing the accounts each month. This involved recruiting me and my sister to add up lines of numbers and filling in the totals at the bottom and then checking each other's work.

By the time my sister and I were woken up to get ready for school in the morning, my parents would have already done two up-and-back transfers between Brisbane and the Gold Coast, and for these years, in the 1980s and early 1990s, their lives were consumed with serving their customers – Japanese tourists – which was a niche that was booming at that time. Their only competition was Hawaii.

So, while I am now ever grateful to my parents for role-modelling what 'hard work' looks like, my story is not one from hardship, poverty or loss to overcoming seemingly insurmountable hurdles.

Rather, I come from privilege. I was schooled in the best private school in the state (we wore ties and blazers and hats and stockings), I learned an instrument from when I was four, was raised bilingual and learned two more languages in high school because my mother always said 'languages are important'.

While I took this at face value, it wouldn't take long for me to experience the true richness of what language can bring and the depth of cultural immersion it invites. My life has, so far, been incredibly rich because I have been able to participate in the humour of other cultures and languages, and it is humour, I have learned, that forms the core of deep connections.

But coming from an upbringing where your parents give you every opportunity to be successful also has its challenges. And without seeming ungrateful, for me, it was learning the art of managing expectations at a very early age to ease the pressures that I felt. I yearned to be independent, and I still think today that if I could have been independent at twelve, I would have been. I was desperate to make my own decisions, to be able to take responsibility for these decisions, to learn by doing and not have to accept what I was told to do and not do.

I was restless, bored and craved sugar (which was forbidden in our house). I was always decisive, and at fourteen, I decided I wanted to be a pharmacist. This became the centre of my focus for the next three years as I studied every waking minute to get the score needed to get into pharmacy. Somehow, I scraped it in, and this was the beginning of carving out my own path.

To set myself on a path of my choosing was immensely important to me. When I moved out at nineteen, in my third year of uni, I was determined that I would never accept a penny from anyone – especially not my parents. I was determined to never have to hear others make excuses for my achievements because of my 'privileged upbringing'.

It's funny because there are a few quotes that go around which are intended to help people, which I find I can't help but reject. One of those is: 'It's okay to say no.' When we look at this in the context of career building, for me, this is one that must be balanced with hunger. I generally say 'yes' to everything, and while I know this goes against so many points of view today when we are battling social pressures, mental wellbeing and simply coping, for me, saying 'yes' is what has led me to so many incredible learning opportunities and experiences.

My innate character is one that thrives on the threat of change, chaos and even crises, and the chance to take on more presents excitement and anticipation. I am happiest when I am creating and building and in an overdrive mode, and I could say that I am perhaps addicted to the satisfaction that comes with the completion of something that was outside of my comfort zone.

I have spent most of my career outside of my comfort zone,

and with every new job and every new assignment in a new country, I have inevitably felt that 'oh-shit' moment. And this is the moment that drives me forward. I am driven by a fear of failure and motivated by problems.

For an introvert, a major part of feeling uncomfortable is the thought of working with entirely new teams, being the newcomer and serving new customers. Around every corner, I have met the most incredible people, and colleagues have become long-time friends and I have had the opportunity to casually chat and learn from people in so many corners of the world.

We each have our stories, our pasts and futures and are motivated by factors that are so deep within us that even we may struggle to articulate why something is important to us or why we behave a certain way and why our behaviours are different from what we say. This is what is fascinating about us all.

When we layer on cultural nuance, generational beliefs and trends, we find that today's marketers must master the art of uncovering deep human truths and securing the attention of their 'target'. Over the years we have experienced seismic shifts in what marketing is and how it is executed.

There were once three mass channels: TV, radio and print. Today, there are countless channels, and we consume something like 300m of scrolling every day. Our attention spans have diminished from twelve seconds in the year 2000 to three to five seconds twenty years later – now sitting below the average goldfish attention span of nine seconds.

Whilst segmentation has existed throughout time (even my parents had a specific niche market – Japanese honeymooners – because this was the only time a man could take three days off work to travel), the level of segmentation has necessarily become increasingly granular. If we are to catch the attention of those we aim to help, we must be single-minded in how we reach them, communicate with them, engage them and serve them.

My latest endeavours have involved quitting. This has been by far the biggest 'oh-shit' moment of my life. As we travelled and worked in different countries around the globe, it was here in Australia that I met my husband back in 2005.

Given that he had supported every move to every country and sacrificed his own advancement for mine, I was quite nervous about how accepting he might be of this 'quitting' endeavour. My concerns were unfounded, and his support of my need to chase my dreams is something that I feel very lucky to have found in a husband.

Throughout my career, I have toyed with starting my own company. It's in my bloodline, after all. My parents had their own business and both my grandparents on both sides had their own businesses.

My sister and I were the first generation to work for other companies. I had the itch to start a business back in my early twenties, and over the years and decades I not only wrote down many ideas, I wrote business plans, did market research (also via fax using numbers from the phone book) and even sometimes I had stock ready to sell. Each time, I learned new skills in pre-launch marketing, business planning and how to set up companies. But when it came to launching, it all stopped.

This was my fear of failure, and while it has served as a prime motivator for me when working for other companies, it has stalled me in small business. I knew the statistics of failing small businesses, and I feared becoming part of those stats. I was guilty of perhaps over-researching the risks, and the risks that I became aware of became show stoppers. I didn't back my ability to overcome all the hurdles I could see, nor the ones I couldn't. So, none of the ideas saw the light of day, and each one was buried in the graveyard before its birth.

Property in Sydney has, in my memory, always been out of reach, and coming from Brisbane, I soon learned that buying a unit served as a stepping stone to buying a house. Over the years I had thought that a model of buying property together with clear contracts in place for ownership and decision-making would emerge as a way for people to build equity earlier and serve also as a stepping stone, but that has not been the case.

Five years ago, I started investigating this deeper, talking to many lawyers, people in the real estate industry and lenders and understanding all the hurdles and barriers to a structured mortgage-sharing model. It had become of greater interest to me one day when my husband and I were on a road trip in the USA with his daughter.

The deeper I went into the idea and its commercialisation, the more I could see that there were no real show stoppers, just complexities that needed to be navigated. While I didn't have all the answers to all the disastrous what-if scenarios and I struggled to find good solution-oriented lawyers to work with, I decided to go ahead and start building the tech platform for matchmaking that would make co-ownership accessible to anyone who wanted to buy a half or quarter shares of property.

I called it Proppie, as it represented the ability to own a piece of the property pie. For me, it was a great way to get into the nitty-gritty of tech development as there were many learnings I could reapply back to my day job in Japan where we were building an ecommerce business.

We built it slowly over three years, and by the time it was complete, my husband and I had already moved back to Australia, and I was working at Blackmores. It was time for me to make a big decision: to leap into or shelve Proppie. It meant chasing a dream of starting a business and changing the world around me or staying on the corporate course, which I loved.

One thing had changed, and the balance had tipped. The fear of regret now was greater than the fear of failure. Being back in Australia made my business bug itch more than ever, and I found the thought of bringing Proppie to market all-consuming. The news was full of headlines around unaffordable housing, the death of the millennial dream and soaring property prices, and with property prices growing at eleven times wage growth, there was a clear need for a new solution.

Many things had changed since twenty-five years ago, and I would say that even five years ago the market would not have been ready for Proppie. In that time, we have seen not only leaps in technology but a notable shift in the sharing mindset of millennials. The idea of doing things together and sharing for better outcomes has become the new rebellion against the ideas of the baby boomers.

So, while the problem was clear, I needed to give consideration to who, specifically, we would serve. Being specific about the audience and whom we would help allowed us to be very specific in our communication and offering. We would help people to buy property in teams and match owner-occupiers with owner-investors and support them through the process from search to settlement and selling their share. Our market included:

- Parents and their grown children.
- Siblings.
- Friends.
- Couples.
- Parties unknown to each other who were matched.

We made the conscious decision to start broadly with millennials who are known to each other, twenty-five to forty years old, living in Sydney or Melbourne. The idea was to start broad and then narrow in on the most receptive audiences who signed up, as we optimised the conversion funnel and the media channel mix.

We were also aware that there was an adjacent market of those we called 'stayers', and we defined these consumers as people who want to stay in their homes but can't. It would include those who had experienced adverse life events such as divorce or separation, health issues or circumstances that would require them to raise money and use the capital in their home.

The challenge for people at these critical times is that timing may not be their friend if there is the risk that if a property needs to be sold up, they are not able to get back into the market as they may not have sufficient borrowing power or runway for a loan. For this group of people, there is the opportunity to sell part of their property to a co-owner but remain living in the property.

This segment inevitably appeared once we launched as a highly motivated group, and while we treat this as 'spillover' to serve, we consciously decided to not market to this segment during the early years.

Other segments of groups of investors have also emerged, and the temptation to shift content and the user experience to accommodate this group exists.

However, as we look to our purpose as our compass – which is to make home ownership possible for millennials by mortgage-sharing – we will stick to the group of consumers we set out to serve. And as we have learned more over time, we have uncovered which traits are held by the 'innovators' within the segment.

Before a new product can be 'mass', it must first be tried and tested by early adopters – but before the early adopters come the innovators. These innovators, who have specific interests, hobbies and work in specific industries (all filters that can be layered over the original consumer segment) now form the basis of a very tight consumer segment we aim to serve.

It is tempting to set up a segment based on demographics, geography and age, and stop there, but reflecting on all the learnings over the years, I think what I find most interesting about our customer base is getting in deeper with them and understanding where they came from, how they grew up, what they talked about with their parents, whether they discussed property at home, who they turn to for advice, why they want to buy a property and what goal or belief does it fulfil, and then connecting this to data such as where they heard about Proppie and what information they consume, starts to give me a very rich picture and persona of our Proppie consumer.

With this, we can be very specific in how and what we communicate, and we can design feature enhancements and the user experience for them to enjoy, and it's all in the name of helping them with a problem they need help solving.

What's nice about a startup is you get to know every customer, and everything you do is for them. It's not for your boss, it's not for reports and it's not for shareholders. It's only for those we serve – our customers.

AYUMI UYEDA

With an affinity for discovery, Ayumi's path has led her through many cultures and countries, and over time her attraction to solving the unsolvable has become stronger. With deep roots in health care and most recently as the managing director of Blackmores, she has held general management and senior global positions at Bayer in Japan, South East Asia and the USA in consumer health and pharmaceuticals, and has successfully started up ecommerce business models.

Ayumi got her start as a hospital pharmacist in Brisbane, which formed the foundation of her pursuit of health and her belief that 'we are nothing without our health'. She is inspired by problems and is relentless in tackling these in new ways, deriving immense satisfaction from the positive impact that solving such problems can have on people.

Her mission now is to address the housing affordability crisis facing millennials in Australia, and she believes that helping this generation find a path to individual independence will enable them to experience a sense of empowerment, future security and happiness, unlocking the full potential that this generation has to offer. She believes that unless millennials can see that there is a path for them to realise their Aussie dream of home ownership, the risk of 'giving up' on their hopes will set society back substantially. By drawing direct links between the housing crisis and the health and wellbeing of the millennial generation, she aims to solve one problem (the housing affordability crisis) and mitigate an even greater risk of broad-spread mental wellbeing challenges down the track.

Ayumi's depth of corporate experience and starting businesses in new markets sets her up strongly to embark on reshaping the property market with her new startup, Proppie, which is a mortgage-sharing matchmaker platform designed to help millennials to make a start into property by buying in teams.

LETTING YOUR MISSION GUIDE YOUR STRATEGY

Babita Spinelli

Talk to any business consultant about your business plans and the first question they'll ask you is, 'What's your strategy?' If you're like a lot of business owners, your mind will immediately go blank when faced with this question. You might feel the colour drain from your face and your heart start to race as you think to yourself, *Oh no ... what if I don't have a strategy?*

If your anxiety is rising as your confidence is plunging, take a deep breath right now. This chapter is meant to be helpful to you, and I don't want you to lose hope or feel frustrated as you read it. In fact, I know that so many entrepreneurs and small business owners don't have a strategy. I also know that that's absolutely okay!

I don't believe that developing a strategy for your business is the most important thing you should do. Is a strategy helpful? Absolutely. Should you spend time developing one? Definitely.

Will it be the single most important thing you do as a business owner? I don't believe so.

If a strategy isn't the most important thing you can do for your business, then what is?

Good question. In my opinion, your mission statement is even more important than your strategy. Why? Well, we'll get to that. But first, let me say a few more things about your business strategy.

What is a business strategy, anyway?

According to the International Institute for Management Development (IMD), a business strategy is 'a clear set of plans, actions and goals that outlines how a business will compete in a particular market, or markets, with a product or number of products or services'.[1] This organisation goes on to say that a strategy should include several different elements, including things like management, marketing plans, systems and resources.[1] I don't know about you, but that sounds complicated, confusing and overwhelming to me. At least IMD also said that the concept of business strategies is simple enough to understand, the actual implementation of the strategy is (and I quote) 'no easy task'.[1]

Let me share part of my own story with you for a moment.

Being a psychotherapist is my second career. Before that, I was an attorney and high-powered executive working in a Fortune 100 company. For reasons I don't need to share here, I left the corporate world and started training to become a psychotherapist and coach. Fast-forward a few years, and it was time for me to start my own business. *Easy,* I thought. *I worked for a Fortune 100 company. I can do this in my sleep!*

---

1) From *What is business strategy?* 2021, International Institute for Management Development. imd.org/imd-reflections/reflection-page/business-strategy

But I couldn't. When I thought about writing my own business strategy, I would freeze. I didn't even know where to start. I had so many ideas floating in my head, all of which I wanted to take action on, but I knew I couldn't do it all. So, I wondered how I could make this process easier for myself. I began thinking about the core of what I wanted my therapy and coaching business to do – the essence of the work, if you will. I wrote and wrote until I could whittle it into a single sentence – I help create sustainable, positive change in the lives of executives and other successful professionals who struggle to find access to the right kind of support for their experiences.

After more reflection, I realised that this one-sentence statement is the single most important thing I could have written about my business.

What is your *raison d'être*?

The French have a phrase, *raison d'être*, in their language. This simple term translates as 'reason for being'. A quick Google search shows that the phrase means so much more than that. According to Google's English dictionary (provided by Oxford Languages), *raison d'être* is 'the most important reason or purpose for someone or something's existence'.[2]

That's an interesting concept as the most important reason or purpose for someone OR SOMETHING's existence.

We often associate purpose or intention with people, right? We say things like, 'I want to live with intention,' or, 'My purpose in life is to do good.' How often do we think of a business when we talk about purpose? Honestly, not as often as we should.

Let's think about that for a moment. Can you imagine what our world would be like if every single business – every large

---

2) From raison d'etre, 2022, Lexico (Oxford). lexico.com/en/definition/raison_d'etre

corporation, mom-and-pop shop, startup company, solopreneur and non-profit organisation – was guided by its *raison d'être?* Maybe that's too big a vision for us right now, so let's start small. What if *your* business was guided by its *raison d'être?* What would be possible for you then? That's a big question that this chapter will help you find an answer to.

So how *do* you figure out your *raison d'être?*

Good question. If we project this term – *raison d'être* – onto your business, what we're really talking about is your business' reason for existing. We're referring to its meaning, its purpose … its mission.

At its core, your company's mission is its raison d'être.

If we go back to the earlier example of my own process, that single-sentence statement that was the single most important thing I could have written about my business was actually the *raison d'être* for my own practice. Without realising, I had gotten to the heart of my business and crafted a statement that would stand as its mission and guide its strategy.

What is a mission statement?

Let's get technical for a moment, shall we? According to the Society for Human Resource Management (SHRM), a company's mission statement is a short, succinct statement communicating its purpose, intention and reason for existing.[3] *Business News Daily* says that a business' mission statement should include not just what the company does, but also what its values are and the main goal that it's accomplishing.[4]

Think about a company you admire. When you think about

---

[3] From *What is the difference between mission, vision and values statements?* 2022, Society for Human Resource Management. shrm.org/resourcesandtools/tools-and-samples/hr-qa/pages/isthereadifferencebetweenacompany'smission,visionandvaluestatements.aspx

[4] From 'How to create a company mission' by Jennifer Dublino, 2022, *Business News Daily*. businessnewsdaily.com/3783-mission-statement.html

their mission statement, does it leave you feeling inspired? I hope so, because it should.

It should also help you answer some very specific questions about the company, like:

- Why does the company exist?
- Who does the company serve?
- What does the company do?
- What values drive the company?
- What's important to the company?

Now think about your own company. Can you answer all those questions about your own business? Can you answer *any* of those questions about your own business? If you can, great! You're in a good spot! If you can't, that's okay too. Just keep reading, because I'm going to help you get there.

Before we move on, there's one last thing I'd like to say about what a mission statement is. *Business News Daily* offers what I think is a helpful definition about a company's mission statement – according to them, a business' mission statement is 'the founders' most crucial priorities beyond monetary gain'.[5] This simple statement reminds us that companies don't exist just to make money. Well, sure, I guess some do, but are those the companies you want to model your own business after?

Probably not.

If you're like most entrepreneurs, you started your business because you have passion. You want to make a difference in the world. You have a product or service that you think will help create positive change for people. When you harness that mindset,

---

5) From 'How to create a company mission' by Jennifer Dublino, 2022, *Business News Daily*. businessnewsdaily.com/3783-mission-statement.html

you're embracing your company's *raison d'être* and setting the foundation of your mission statement.

Why is a mission statement so important?

A mission statement can be considered 'mission critical' for a company (pun intended). Every company on the planet was started for a specific purpose, but that original purpose can get lost as the business grows and develops. Without realising it, a business owner can unintentionally take their company far away from their *raison d'être* if they're not careful. That's where a mission statement can be so powerful.

In my experience, there are four very distinct ways that a mission statement adds value to a business:

Guides strategy

Your mission statement isn't something that lives on a piece of paper shoved in the back of a desk drawer. In fact, your mission statement makes your business' *raison d'être* come to life. It becomes the heartbeat of your business, guiding and directing the business strategy. Your mission statement will tell you where you're going. Your strategy will tell you how you'll get there.

Business owners can be opportunistic and feel like their business should be able to 'do it all'. In fact, I've fallen into that trap myself as a psychotherapist and coach. But 'doing it all' is a trap that can be harmful to both your business and your wellbeing. In reality, you should have a clear idea in mind of the specifics of what your business does. And this comes straight from your mission.

Influences decision-making

In addition to strategy, your mission has the power to influence everything about your business – growth, hiring, product design, customer experience, even HR policies. In essence, a mission statement serves as a North Star guiding a business every step of the way.

How is this so? you may be asking. Good question.

Your mission is the heartbeat of your company; therefore, it should be considered for every decision you're looking to make …

Want to expand your services? Ask yourself, *What additional services would fall under our mission?*

Looking to grow your team? Ask yourself, *What added role(s) are needed to serve our mission?*

Have to change delivery vendors? Ask yourself, *Which vendors align with our mission and will give our customers an experience we will be proud of?*

If you find yourself struggling with a decision, go back to your mission. What does your mission support? If you're on the fence about a decision, ask if it falls within the boundaries of your mission … that's how your mission statement can be your 'North Star'.

Puts boundaries around your products and services

One of my favourite questions to ask business owners to reflect on is, 'Just because you can, does that mean you should?' As I mentioned earlier, entrepreneurs and small business owners are notorious for trying to 'do it all', but trying to be everything to everyone can actually diffuse valuable resources and become a barrier to success.

Here's a helpful example:

Acme Consulting Group wants to be the 'leading authority on employee engagement for small to mid-size organisations'. Their mission says they 'help everyday leaders cultivate engaged employees to optimise talent and make a difference in their community.' The company's founder recently met the CEO of a large multinational technology corporation, who wants Acme Consulting Group to help streamline leadership operations for the executive team. What should this founder do?

As exciting as this project is to the founder, it's not an automatic yes. The founder should go back to the mission statement for Acme Consulting Group and see how this project would advance the mission – will streamlining leadership operations for the executive team of a large multinational technology corporation 'help everyday leaders cultivate engaged employees to optimise talent and make a difference in their community'? Probably not. So as tempting as this opportunity is, it's not aligned with the company's mission.

When you find yourself falling into the trap of wanting to 'do it all', I want you to go straight to that question, 'Just because we can, does that mean we should?' Just like in this example, your mission statement can help you uncover the answer to that question which will allow you to put necessary boundaries around your products or services.

Tell your stakeholders who you are

There are so many factors that go into a successful business beyond its mission and strategy, like its culture. Well, guess what? Culture is also driven by a mission. In fact, *Business News Daily* asserts that a company's culture starts with a 'defined, tangible mission'.[6]

Why is this important? Well, having a strong culture that is built on a 'defined, tangible mission' helps demonstrate to your key stakeholders who you really are as a company. Everyone from

---

6) From 'How to create a company mission' by Jennifer Dublino, 2022, *Business News Daily*. businessnewsdaily.com/3783-mission-statement.html

your company leaders, employees, contractors, board members and even your customers or client base will know what to expect from you when they know what your mission and culture are.

This is especially important when it comes to internal stakeholders, like employees and contractors. Having a mission and a strong sense of company culture sets the tone for critical employee factors that will help improve your company's overall performance, like engagement, buy-in, loyalty and retention.

Case study

I'd like to use one of my favourite mission-driven organisations, Warby Parker, to illustrate the value of a company's mission statement. Warby Parker is a popular eyewear company founded in 2010 by four college friends in an effort to solve a massive problem in the world: the high cost of eyewear.

On their website, Warby Parker states that their mission is to 'inspire and impact the world with vision, purpose and style'.[7] Twelve years into their endeavour, the four friends have grown the business to a multimillion-dollar company that has, according to experts, 'disrupted' an industry that had a monopoly on the manufacturing, sales and distribution of eyewear in the US, unwavering in their mission.[8]

Since its early years, Warby Parker has defined itself by three simple things, 1) affordable and stylish eyewear, 2) fun customer experiences and 3) making an impact through its 'Buy a Pair, Give a Pair' program.[7]

When we break down its mission statement, we can see each of those focal points supports its mission.

---

7) From Warby Parker website, 2022. warbyparker.com/history
8) From 'What's behind Warby Parker's success?' by Stephanie Denning, 2016, *Forbes*. forbes.com/sites/stevedenning/2016/03/23/whats-behind-warby-parkers-success/?sh=2215db9e411a

- Affordable and stylish eyewear = 'inspire and impact the world with vision, purpose and style'.
- Fun customer experiences = 'inspire and impact the world with vision, purpose and style'.
- Make an impact = 'inspire and impact the world with vision, purpose and style'.

In 2019, Warby Parker expanded its product offerings to include contact lenses. Let's look at that decision through the 'just because we can, does that mean we should?' question.

Were contact lenses as a product part of their original strategic plan? Unlikely.

Did contact lenses as a product require significant changes to key business factors like manufacturing, marketing and sales? Definitely.

Do contact lenses as a product help them continue to impact the world with vision, purpose and style? Absolutely.

Has adding contact lenses as a product helped them impact even more people in the world? Without a doubt.

This is a prime example of when a company had a decision to make and chose to make a notable strategic shift *in support of their mission.*

As a quick caveat to this case study, it's possible that Warby Parker actually changed their mission statement. In my research for this chapter, I found several references that noted their mission statement as, 'to offer designer eyewear at a revolutionary price, while leading the way for socially conscious businesses'.[9] However, I could not find this statement *anywhere* on their website. My hunch is that they changed it from this to the current mission statement – 'to inspire and impact the world with vision, purpose

---

9) From Mission Statement website, 2022. mission-statement.com/warby-parker

and style' – when they decided to expand their products to include contact lenses. If that's the case, this is a great example of a company that kept the essence of its original mission but expanded the language to allow for even greater impact in the world.

Other mission statements

Though Warby Parker is one of my favourites, they aren't the only mission-driven organisation out there. Here are some other mission statements from well-known companies to inspire and motivate you:

Service-based companies:
- American Red Cross: To prevent and alleviate human suffering in the face of emergencies by mobilising the power of volunteers and the generosity of donors.[10]
- Universal Health Services, Inc: To provide superior quality health care services that: patients recommend to family and friends, physicians prefer for their patients, purchasers select for their clients, employees are proud of and investors seek for long-term returns.[11]
- Starbucks: To inspire and nurture the human spirit – one person, one cup and one neighbourhood at a time.[12]
- Tripadvisor: To help people around the world plan and have the perfect trip.[10]

Product-based companies:
- Swarovski Crystals: Swarovski adds sparkle to everyday

---

10) From *51 mission statement examples from the world's best companies*, Alessio Bresciani, 2022. alessiobresciani.com/foresight-strategy/51-mission-statement-examples-from-the-worlds-best-companies
11) From *27 mission and vision statement examples that will inspire your buyers* by Lindsay Kolowich Cox, 2022, Hubspot. blog.hubspot.com/marketing/inspiring-company-mission-statements
12) From *17 seriously inspiring mission and vision statement examples* by Thomas Law, 2021, Oberlo. oberlo.com/blog/inspiring-mission-vision-statement-examples

life with high-quality products and services that exceed our customers' desires. We inspire our colleagues with innovation and reward their achievements while striving to expand our market leadership.[13]
- Patagonia: Build the best product, cause no unnecessary harm, use business to inspire and implement solutions to the environmental crisis.[14]
- IKEA: To offer a wide range of well-designed, functional home furnishing products at prices so low that as many people as possible will be able to afford them.[15]
- ASOS: To become the number-one fashion destination for twenty-somethings globally.[15]

Technology-based companies:
- LinkedIn: To connect the world's professionals to make them more productive and successful.[15]
- Instagram: To capture and share the world's moments.[16]
- Prezi: To reinvent how people share knowledge, tell stories and inspire their audiences to act.[17]
- Adobe: To move the web forward and give web designers and developers the best tools and services in the world.[14]

Developing your own mission statement

I hope after reading this far, you realise how critical it is for your business. So, here's the big question, are you ready to start

---

13) From *How to write a powerful business mission statement (+15 examples)* by Nahla Davies, 2021, Wordstream by LocaliQ. wordstream.com/blog/ws/2021/07/02/how-to-write-a-business-mission-statement

14) From *17 seriously inspiring mission and vision statement examples* by Thomas Law, 2021, Oberlo. oberlo.com/blog/inspiring-mission-vision-statement-examples

15) From Mission Statement website, 2022. mission-statement.com/ikea

16) From Mission Statement website, 2022. mission-statement.com/instagram

17) From *27 mission and vision statement examples that will inspire your buyers* by Lindsay Kolowich Cox, 2022, Hubspot. blog.hubspot.com/marketing/inspiring-company-mission-statements

developing your own mission statement now?

If you're a little nervous to get started, that's okay.

One reason you might be nervous is because people tend to make their mission statement complicated when it doesn't need to be. In fact, it shouldn't be complicated. Your mission statement should be simple, specific, clear, direct and concise.[18] It should also be compelling and relevant to your work.

As you begin to dive in, keep in mind that your first draft doesn't have to be perfect. In fact, you'll find that most companies go through several rounds of mission statements before they find the perfect one.

Here are some thought-provoking questions to reflect on, along with an example from the mission statements above for each question, that can help you start to develop your mission statement:

- What is your *why*? As in, why did you start your company?
  Example: I started mine to give executives and other high-power professionals a safe space to do their own self-development work.
- What problem does your company solve?
  Example: Warby Parker's founders felt that eyeglasses were too expensive. So, they created Warby Parker to provide lower-cost options for eyewear.[19]
- What is the number-one most important thing to you as it relates to your company?
  Example: IKEA values value … their products are designed to be low cost, so everything they do is with not only functionality but price in mind so they can offer 'prices so low that as many

---

18) From *How to write a mission statement* by Sally Lauckner, 2020, Nerd Wallet. nerdwallet.com/article/small-business/how-to-write-a-mission-statement
19) From Warby Parker website, 2022. warbyparker.com/history

people as possible will be able to afford them'.[20]
- What sets your business apart from other similar businesses?
Example: Patagonia is very environmentally driven, which creates a specific niche for them in the outdoor apparel and equipment market.[21]
- Who do you want to work with or sell to?
Example: Adobe calls out web designers and developers in their mission statement. Their products are used by people who don't fall into those roles, but they are designed with those specific people in mind.[22]
- Who do you not want to work with or sell to?
Example: ASOS specifically says they want to be the number-one fashion destination for twenty-somethings. By their mission, we know their products aren't designed with older people in mind.[24]
- What do you want your business to be known for?
Example: Tripadvisor is known for being one of the go-to places on the internet for advice about trips, which is precisely what their mission statement wants!

I know it can feel intimidating to try to craft your mission statement. You're so passionate about what you do, you might be wondering, *Where do I even start?* After reflecting on the questions above, here is a basic template to help get you started ...

1. Who does it? – This is usually I or We.
2. What action do you do? – This can be simple like provide, sell, offer, help, create.

---

20) From Mission Statement website, 2022. mission-statement.com/ikea
21) From *17 seriously inspiring mission and vision statement examples* by Thomas Law, 2021, Oberlo. oberlo.com/blog/inspiring-mission-vision-statement-examples
22) From *51 mission statement examples from the world's best companies* by Alessio Bresciani, 2022. alessiobresciani.com/foresight-strategy/51-mission-statement-examples-from-the-worlds-best-companies

3. Who do you do it for? – This is where you would identify your ideal client.
4. What results do you get? – This is where you mention what your customer or client gets out of it.
5. How do you do it? – This is where you can set yourself apart from your competition.

If I were to use this template on my own business, I would come up with this mission statement:

I help executives and other successful professionals create sustainable, positive change in their lives by providing high-quality coaching and therapy services that are accessible and understanding of their personal and professional experiences.

Find a community for support

Whether you're just starting out or you've been in business for decades, it's never too late to write your mission statement. If you haven't done so already, I encourage you to set some time aside for this before you go any further in your business. And if you find yourself stuck, there are lots of resources for support. You can research other mission-based businesses for benchmarking or join a local networking group. Or you can look to coaches and mastermind groups for professional guidance. Another option is working with a mentor who can offer support and feedback.

The bottom line is that you don't have to figure this out by yourself. Reach out for support when you need it, ask for feedback from others and keep in mind that your mission will likely go through several drafts before it's finished. That's all part of the process and to be expected when you're taking your dream and turning it into a mission-driven organisation!

Appendix

- Bresciani, A (n.d.). *51 mission statement examples from the world's best companies*. Alessio Bresciani. Retrieved 17 April 2022 from alessiobresciani.com/foresight-strategy/51-mission-statement-examples-from-the-worlds-best-companies
- Cox, L K (9 March 2022). *27 mission and vision statement examples that will inspire your buyers*. HubSpot Blog. Retrieved 17 April 2022 from blog.hubspot.com/marketing/inspiring-company-mission-statements
- Davies, N (9 December 2021). *15 business mission statement examples & HOW TO WRITE YOURS*. WordStream. Retrieved 17 April 2022 from wordstream.com/blog/ws/2021/07/02/how-to-write-a-business-mission-statement
- Denning, S (30 June 2021). *What's behind Warby Parker's success?* Forbes. Retrieved 17 May 2022 from forbes.com/sites/stevedenning/2016/03/23/whats-behind-warby-parkers-success/?sh=2215db9e411a
- Dublino, J (3 March 2022). *How to create a company mission*. Business News Daily. Retrieved 17 April 2022 from businessnewsdaily.com/3783-mission-statement.html
- *History*. Warby Parker. (n.d.). Retrieved 17 April 2022 from warbyparker.com/history
- *IKEA mission statement 2022: IKEA Mission & Vision Analysis*. IKEA Mission Statement 2022 | IKEA Mission & Vision Analysis. (27 January 2021). Retrieved 17 April 2022 from mission-statement.com/ikea
- *Instagram mission statement analysis*. Instagram Mission Statement Analysis. (22 October 2021). Retrieved 17 April 2022 from mission-statement.com/instagram
- Lauckner, S (11 September 2020). *How to write A mission statement (infographic)*. NerdWallet. Retrieved

17 April 2022 from nerdwallet.com/article/small-business/how-to-write-a-mission-statement
- Law, T J (9 April 2022). *17 mission and vision statement examples to follow in 2022.* Oberlo. Retrieved 17 April 2022 from oberlo.com/blog/inspiring-mission-vision-statement-examples
- Lexico Dictionaries. (n.d.). *Raison d'être English definition and meaning.* Lexico Dictionaries | English. Retrieved 17 April 2022 from lexico.com/en/definition/raison_d'etre
- Mainwaring, S (2 December 2020). *Purpose at work: Warby Parker's keys to Success.* Forbes. Retrieved 17 April 2022 from forbes.com/sites/simonmainwaring/2020/12/01/purpose-at-work-warby-parkers-keys-to-success/?sh=56662ab6dba7+https%3A%2F%2Fwww.imd.org%2Fimd-reflections%2Freflection-page%2Fbusiness-strategy%2F
- Society for Human Resource Management. (n.d.). *What is the difference between mission, vision and values statements?* sham.org. Retrieved 18 April 2022 from shrm.org/resourcesandtools/tools-and-samples/hr-qa/pages

BABITA SPINELLI

Babita Spinelli is an internationally recognised award-winning psychotherapist, executive coach, mental health consultant and relationship expert. She focuses on helping people optimise their relationships and thrive in their lives. Babita also works with heart-centred businesses to help them grow and be successful while leading their organisations effectively.

As a former lawyer and Wall Street executive, Babita also brings a unique perspective to managing mental health issues and relationships in the workplace, developing business strategy relating to human dynamics and resolving high-conflict issues. Her corporate background and experience are key to partnering with executives and leaders who recognise the benefit of a holistic approach to lead their organisations and to navigate the unique challenges they face in the workplace, in their personal lives and in their relationships. In her private practice and public engagements, she empowers people and organisations to examine and redefine relationships as a tool for personal and professional growth.

Babita Spinelli is a sought-after human relations expert in media across the globe and has been featured in over a hundred media outlets such as *Forbes,* Bloomberg, ABC, NBC, CNN, *Men's Health, Oprah Magazine, Business Insider, Huffington Post, The Washington Post,* SXSW and Mind Body Green. Babita Spinelli is a recipient of the 2022 Prestige Award for Psychotherapist of the Year, the 2019 New York Psychotherapist Award and was named one of New Jersey's top ten women entrepreneurs in 2020. Babita Spinelli is also a 2022 SXSW speaker and serves as an advisory board member of Speak As One raising mental health awareness and breaking the stigma through stories.

Education/Certifications
- New York University.
- Temple University School of Law.
- National Institute for the Psychotherapies (NIP) – Five-year psychoanalytic training program.
- Coach Training Alliance executive coaching.
- New Jersey Collaborative Divorce certification.
- Gottman Institute certified educator & facilitator of new parents/parenting.
- EMDRAEMDR Trauma Training level one and two certified.

CREATING A UNIQUE VALUE PROPOSITION

Dr Adama Kalokoh

One of my all-time favourite animated movies is *The Lion King* because it is filled with many life lessons that I still apply today. My favourite part of the movie is a scene with Rafiki, the baboon, as he leads Simba to the spirit of his father, Mufasa. Simba is reminded of a great life principle by his father, 'Remember who you are.'

This line has stuck with me for the longest time and has been a driving inspiration for my leadership growth. There is greatness inside all of us meaning there are unique skills, strengths, experiences and valuable attributes that set us apart from each other. Knowing these unique skills will position you to reach your greatest leadership potential.

We are uniquely designed for greatness ... there are no two persons alike. Our value stems from our unique shape, experiences, skill sets and background. We all have something to bring to the table, but knowing what you bring to the table is key. If you don't know your value, then no-one will really recognise your value or worth.

Creating a unique value proposition focuses on developing clear statements and goals that describe the benefit of your skill sets and strengths, how you can solve the customers' needs, or in other cases, the needs of a particular company and what distinguishes you from the competition.

Your unique value proposition should be very clear and be part of your brand as a global leader. In this chapter, I am so excited to share my journey to leadership and how this key life principle has helped me become a global woman leader, know who I am and the value I bring.

As I begin this chapter, I must remind you once again that I had to 'remember who I was' to dive into what was inside of me, therefore becoming the true woman leader I was always destined to be.

My name is Dr Adama Kalokoh, proud African-American woman living in the DC metropolitan area born in the US to parents from Sierra Leone, West Africa.

I am the founder and director of Impact Sierra Leone, an NGO with several projects in West Africa. Our mission is to reduce socioeconomic challenges in Sierra Leone through empowerment, education and building strong partnerships with the Diaspora community. Allow me to share a bit of my journey of discovery which led me to tapping into my greatest qualities and skills.

I have always had a passion for helping others and international development. My parents instilled in me a deep sense of pride and appreciation for my Sierra Leonean heritage. As a former active-duty member of the US Air Force who honourably served for four years, I learned the value of making great connections with people of all races and to embrace diversity. The military brought out skills in me I never knew existed. The military taught me keen leadership and organisational skills that would later be a great benefit to my future career. I completed my undergraduate studies at the University of the District of Columbia and graduated with a Bachelor of Science in Health Education. During my junior year of college, I received a scholarship from the Thurgood Marshall Foundation and was introduced to the Gallup Foundation. They gave each of us a copy of the *StrengthsFinder 2.0, Discover Your CliftonStrengths* by Don Clifton. This book truly transformed my thinking because I learned the value of focusing on my strengths and using them to grow in my professional development. I encourage each of you to read this book and take the StrengthsFinder assessment. Often, we focus on our weaknesses and develop new skills rather than tapping into our current strengths and talents.

Simon T Bailey once stated, 'It's not who you are that holds you back from brilliant success, it's who you think you're not that holds you back.' Sometimes, we focus on who we think we're not instead of who we are. After taking the StrengthsFinder assessment, I learned my greatest strengths are communication, empathy, motivating others and team building.

These attributes would later propel me into my greatest destiny. Now, my strength in communication was a bit of a challenge because I had a huge fear of public speaking.

However, over time as my passion for service developed, this fear would eventually diminish. One of my favourite points in the book states, 'You cannot be anything you want to be – but you can be a lot more of who you already are.' This was so very important to my growth, recognising my strengths and abilities as a leader and motivator.

Upon conclusion of my college education, I began volunteer work with Americorps (2001-2003) as a volunteer director and was inducted into the Americorps Promise Fellowship. My Americorps experience positioned me as a leader by serving as volunteer director, managing hundreds of volunteers monthly throughout the DMV. Leadership led me to reach thousands of marginalised people at soup kitchens, shelters and schools in the DC area. However, there was a significant life experience that was a bigger motivation for me. It was the death of my father that motivated me to be a servant leader in Sierra Leone. He loved his motherland and inspired us children to do the same. This deep appreciation led me to finally visit Sierra Leone in 2003, followed by several consecutive visits.

My passion for helping others and devotion to service has elevated me to serve on many board groups impacting Sierra Leone. Additionally, my status as a first generation born West-African positioned me with having unique skills to be a leader in international development. I could serve as a bridge between the US and Africa and be a powerful force!

Now, this leads me to highlight another great scene from *The Lion King* where Mufasa is sharing some valuable tips with his son, Simba. Mufasa states, 'We are all connected in the great circle of life.' No matter who you are – your status, religion, sex – we all deserve the same basic human rights and to be treated with respect. This theme would later become the motto for my NGO, 'United We Stand, and Together We Rise'.

I never knew growing up that my cultural heritage would lead me to being a woman leader and find my true purpose. My purpose and passion have truly become my power. Believe it or not, I was once ashamed of my culture and heritage. My parents, James Conteh and Harriett Memuna Sesay, migrated here in the late seventies looking to better themselves and achieve the 'American dream'.

Like many of their fellow Sierra Leonean counterparts, they sought to make a name for themselves within the African community. As I look back, I got my first taste of humanitarian service from my parents as a little girl. I can still remember the Saturday gatherings at our place with many of my aunts and uncles coming together under the group called Sacoma. This group really served as a network for all the Sierra Leone migrants to the DC area that were particularly from Yonibana. My father was an active member and always believed you should help those who were less fortunate.

Our household did not escape the traditions of our country. Both of my parents retained their deep accents, their culture to include music and beliefs. Every Saturday, the record player was spinning with African oldies while mom prepared the delicious soup for the day. Our favourite was always groundnut soup or potato leaves complimented with sweet plantains. Naturally, they ensured to pass all of the culture on to their American-born children – whether we fully accepted this passed-down culture was another story!

So, here I was, growing up in the Washington DC area, a melting pot of diversity – or so I thought. However, it is where I experienced some of the ugliest hatred for colour among my own African-American people. During my childhood days in school, it became evident that being 'dark-skinned' was not popular. It seemed that if you were light in complexion with 'good' textured hair, you were in the cool kid club. It would be years later that I realised there is no such thing as good hair and that our true beauty comes from within.

Nonetheless, I started to believe that being dark-skinned was not good enough. So, as a result of these negative labels and lots of teasing, I grew up feeling less beautiful and was not excited about being of African descent. I no longer enjoyed my mother's traditional braiding hairstyles or dressing up in traditional outfits. I wanted so much to fit into the American crowd and spare myself any more embarrassment.

Unfortunately, as a result, I wanted to erase any connection with Africa because I truly felt my black was not beautiful. I was very ashamed of who I was in physical appearance, and as a result, I was silent for many years, always finding comfort in my shyness. I did not realise my value or allow my talents to be exposed to the world. I was scarred by past insults and insecurities and decided I did not matter in society.

Now, many years and lots of maturity later, I can say that my negative thinking has drastically changed. With open arms, I accept my culture, my background, my genetic make-up and my dark skin as the essence of my beauty! Many life experiences, such as my enlistment into the United States Air Force and the death of my beloved father in 1997, made my heart realise what my parents said was true.

My parents, especially my father, always reminded me that Africa is my home and I need to make sure that I return home before I leave the Earth. They reminded me that I should always be proud of where I come from and appreciate knowing my African roots. Little did I know this was the beginning of a journey of my global brand as a leader! There is another scene in *The Lion King* where Rafiki is reminding Simba to not dwell in the past but to look toward the future. Here are two of his quotes that I have cherished over the years:

'You are more than what you have become.'

And, 'You can either run from the past ... or learn from it.'

With my service in the military and Americorps, I soon discovered that I was great at making connections while inspiring many around the world. I became a strong advocate for women and girls in Sierra Leone. Due to my in-depth experience in volunteerism and community service and my personal journey as a woman, I felt a great sense of responsibility and inspiration to become an ambassador and agent of change for young girls and women in Sierra Leone.

I have insight on gender issues both in the United States and in West Africa. There seems to be a common factor between the two regions and that is there are far less opportunities for women as compared to men. The playing field has yet to be levelled because we see too often that a woman's skills or experiences are considered less important than her gender. As a global leader, I join in the fight against injustices, stereotypes, discrimination and inhumanity due to gender by promoting empowerment programs. By empowering other women to have a voice, we are impacting the future generation of leaders who will ensure a world of inclusivity and equality where all are valued.

In 2019, after letting go of my fear of failure, I launched 'Impact Sierra Leone' so I could better serve communities at greater capacities. I have made great impact, and at the same time, I worked to sensitise, uplift and reinforce women in Sierra Leone to role models as 'actors of change.'

Over time I realised that one should never stop growing in their development. I soon learned the benefits of social media in networking and connecting. I decided to use social media to tell my story, and in doing so realised I was a powerful female empowerment leader.

I was uniquely designed to be a voice for women around the globe. After many years of wondering what my purpose was, it was crystal clear that I needed to use my skills and strengths to empower, uplift, inspire and transform the minds of those in extreme poverty with focus on Sierra Leone.

During this time, I sought out like-minded leaders via several social media platforms and built many great relationships. I also embraced the one thing I feared so much which was public speaking. I realised that to impact lives, especially women and girls, I needed to be their voice, speaking and sharing their story. I began doing monthly motivation videos to inspire others. I found a lot of inspiration from other female empowerment leaders.

There are three key female leaders who inspired me. Firstly, poet and actress Maya Angelou, whose iconic poems transformed many – her poems *And Still I Rise* and *Phenomenal Woman* have carried me through the worst situations. Secondly, the singer Miriam Makeba, also known as 'Mama Africa', who sang melodic songs filled with strength, bravery, determination and heartfelt emotion. These were pivotal during South African's apartheid movement. Finally, Oumou Sangare, the Mousoulou singer and musician who empowered women in male-dominated societies of Mali. All of these women taught me the value of using my voice to tell the story and impacting lives for the better.

Since then, I have been honoured and received recognition in Sierra Leone and the US from several organisations. I was named the 2019 Yonibana brand ambassador, female empowerment entrepreneur selected as a 2019 Global Goodwill Ambassador and currently serving as chairperson, was among the Top 100 Recognised Human Rights Defenders in the United Nations 2019 Almanac. I was also recognised as the 2019 Diasporan of the Year by the Yoni Excellence Association (YEA) for tireless efforts in reducing poverty through various projects while promoting the beauty of Yonibana.

I was recently nominated and won a medal from the Federation of International Gender and Human Rights in the category of 'Children's Aid and Help'. In addition, in late 2021, I was named one of the recipients of the Dr Nina L Meyerhof Leadership Award for her humanitarian work. This award recognises outstanding individuals who dedicate their lives to bring positive social change and devote their time to fight poverty and injustice and whose accomplishments are consistent with Jacobs-Abbey Global Institute for Leadership Studies goals.

In addition, my commanding personality has made me a natural for hosting a series of successful fundraising events through collaboration with the community association and church organisations in the DC area between 2004 and 2020. I hope to continue serving humanity through my missionary works, impacting Sierra Leone and beyond.

John Quincy Adams once quoted, 'If your actions inspire others to dream more, learn more, do more and become more, you are a leader.' The once shy, insecure girl who had nothing to say has become Dr Adama Kalokoh, a global humanitarian, Global Goodwill Ambassadors Foundation (GGAF) chairperson, SDG advocate, motivational speaker, women's empowerment leader, founder of Impact Sierra Leone and named one of the Most Distinguished Women Change Makers in Africa 2020-2021. This award recognises African women changemakers who are excelling in a multitude of fields and industries.

I have contributed meaningfully to the fields of education, agriculture and health for vulnerable populations in my ancestral village. I chose, as my primary focus, to support women and girls in rural areas because of their huge lack of resources and access to services. I place myself in their shoes because had my mom never travelled to America, I would be born and bred in Sierra Leone.

My current efforts include directly supporting the Foindu village community located in rural Sierra Leone with educational tools, clothing donations and support for farming activities. I launched the Seeds of Life project in March 2019 to combat hunger amongst primary school children in the village.

I committed myself to promoting the United Nations Sustainable Development Goals (SDGs) within my organisation and doing my part to reduce poverty. Using my passion for public health, we launched the Seeds of Life project to help over 250 primary school children access fruits and vegetables and learn about wellness. Due to the sacrifices of women who came before me, I found my voice as a leader and have been fortunate enough to be in a position of leadership and influence.

To honour them, I am using my platform to improve the lives of women and children around me and in Sierra Leone through my organisation, Impact Sierra Leone. I have been able to provide communities in Sierra Leone with hope and inspiration by giving them a voice, meeting them where they are and working with them to improve their lives and outlook on life. Some of the initiatives include starting a school farm for students in the rural community of Foindu village in Sierra Leone and creating an initiative called Seeds Of Life. This initiative focuses on empowerment, enrichment and education activities.

Building on this initiative, we are in the process of implementing a school feeding program, renovating the school and starting a literacy program that will benefit the students and entire community. We will also be launching a skills training program for young women and girls in the near future. Through the Seeds of Life project, we have established four farm sites growing various crops such as groundnuts, okra, pineapples and so much more.

None of these projects would be possible if it were not for

the support from other women on my team who see the value in making sure that women have a voice and a seat at the table when decisions are made on the local, national and international levels.

My dream is to launch empowerment centres in several underserved communities where individuals can learn skills and become entrepreneurs in tailoring, craftwork, shoemaking, hair-braiding, catering, floral design, quilt-making, computer technology and more! I hope that my mission will inspire other descendants of Africa to embrace their culture and positively impact their home country by using their voices and skills to transform communities as well.

I'd like to share my top twelve pieces of advise that have helped shape my unique value proposition:

1. Brand yourself as a leader. There is a leader in all of us, pull out the 'I will' in your life.
2. Know your value and worth. We all have something to bring to the table; always look for ways to add value to an organisation, project or program.
3. Enhance your skills. Use every day to get better and better.
4. Transform your thinking. Attitude is everything; focus on the positives.
5. Network with purpose. Look for ways to exchange ideas and resources and not just take.
6. Find joy in your journey (compete only with yourself – no competition, just collaboration).
7. Keep growing in your professional development. Research your field and see who is doing what you want to do well.
8. Think outside of the box. Creativity is a gift, use it!
9. Become a mentor and a mentee. Learning from others is key.
10. Use social media for good. Be consistent in your messaging

and brand yourself. Be inspiring with your content and practice random messages of kindness. Tell your story and create motivational videos. Seek other connections that are doing similar work and take advantage of free events and webinars that allow you to meet others in your field.
11. Use your voice and make a roar. Your voice matters – find platforms where you can speak and hear other speakers.
12. Plan for your success. Get organised with a notebook, write down all your skills and goals. Apply the SMART goals method – specific, measurable, achievable, relevant and time-bound.
13. Stay motivated to succeed. Don't get bored; get inspired by quotes and other leaders in your field.

I want to end this chapter by recalling a great part of *The Lion King* movie where Mufasa reminds his son that he is a powerful king and stands on the shoulders of kings: 'Look at the stars, the great kings of the past … Remember when you feel alone, the kings will always be there to guide you.' There are two special kings that have passed away who are very dear to me: my father, James I Conteh, and my younger brother, Musa George Conteh. They are a huge inspiration in my life service to others and I carry them with me always on my journey. They were not fortunate to reach their potential in life, so it is my duty to help others reach their potential as a way to honour them. I am reminded of this, that I am a powerful African queen standing on the shoulders of great men and women of the past.

There is greatness in me and therefore, I can do great things as a leader. My voice is my power, and I can transform the minds of many by just using my voice. By empowering minds, we can raise a generation of leaders who will use their skills and strengths to impact their communities in a great way. These leaders will become valuable members of society and boost economic development in their communities. I remind each of you to stand in your greatness, your power, your passion, your purpose, and know that you are a valuable member of your communities.

My favourite insect is the butterfly because it goes through a transformation to become something greater. It begins its journey in a humble state as a caterpillar, and over time, with patience and nature's nectar, it grows beautiful wings that help it to soar to the highest heights. Just like the butterfly, we were born to thrive and not just survive in this world. No matter your story, you are equipped with unique talents and skills to succeed – use everything inside of you as your wings to soar above to the greatest height of success. Keep soaring and remember your worth! I hope you are inspired to look within and embrace those unique skills that will set you apart from others in your field. Work towards your professional development each and every day and inspire the world!

DR ADAMA KALOKOH

Dr Adama Kalokoh, a proud descendant of Sierra Leone, has always had a passion for helping others and international development. Her parents instilled in her a deep sense of pride and appreciation for their Sierra Leonean heritage. As a former active-duty member of the US Air Force who honourably served for four years, Dr Kalokoh is a strong advocate for women and girls in Sierra Leone. She hopes that her mission will inspire other descendants of Africa to embrace their culture and positively impact their home country.

Dr Kalokoh completed her undergraduate studies at the University of the District of Colombia majoring in public health. She holds a Bachelor of Science in health education. Upon conclusion of her education, Adama began volunteerism work with

Americorps (2001-2003) as a volunteer director. She was inducted into the Americorps Promise Fellowship. Her leadership led her to reach thousands of marginalised people at soup kitchens, shelters and schools in the DC area.

But her passion for Sierra Leone became a driving force. This deep appreciation led Adama to finally visit Sierra Leone in 2003, followed by three consecutive visits. Her passion for helping others and devotion to service has elevated her to serve on many board groups impacting Sierra Leone. She is the founder of Impact Sierra Leone, an organisation founded to reduce socioeconomic challenges through empowerment, education and building strong partnerships with the Diaspora community. Due to her experience in volunteerism, she felt a great sense of responsibilty and inspiration to become an ambassador and agent of change for young girls and women in Sierra Leone. At the same time, she is working to sensitise, uplift and reinforce women in Sierra Leone to role model as 'actors of change'.

Dr Kalokoh has contributed meaningfully to the fields of education, agriculture and health for vulnerable populations in her ancestral village. She chose, as a primary focus, to help support women and girls in rural areas because of their huge lack of resources and access to services.

Her current efforts include directly supporting the Foindu village community located in rural Sierra Leone with eductaional tools, clothes donations and support for farming activities. She launched the Seeds of Life project in March 2019 to combat hunger amongst primary school children in the village. She has committed herslef to promoting the United Nations Sustainable Development Goals (SDGs) within her organisation and doing her part to reduce poverty. Using her passion for public health, she launched the Seeds of Life project to help over 250 primary school children access fruits and vegetables and learn about wellness. She has been honoured and received recognition in Sierra Leone and the US as the Yonibana brand ambassador, female empowerment entrepreneur, 2019 Yoni Excellence Diasporan of the Year, 2019 DDEA Humanitarian Recipient, chosen as a 2019 Global Goodwill Ambassador, was among the Top 100 Recognised Human Rights Defenders in the United Nations 2019 Almanac. She received the 2021 Nina L Meyerhof Leadership Award for humanitarian service. This award recognises outstanding individuals who dedicate their lives to bring positive social change and devote their time to fight poverty, injustice and whose accomplishments are consistent with Jacobs-Abbey Global Institute for Leadership Studies' goals.

In addition, her commanding personality has made her a natural for hosting a series of successful fundraising events through collaboration with the community association and church organisations in the DC area between 2004 and 2020. She hopes to continue serving humanity through her missionary works and launch several other projects that promote literacy, public health, enhanced education, empowerment, mentorship and more that will bring lasting solutions to poverty issues. She hopes to grow Impact Sierra Leone into a global brand that will transform the lives of many.

LEVERAGING TECHNOLOGY TO DOMINATE THE BUSINESS ECOSYSTEM

Dr Ingrid Vasiliu-Feltes

All industrial revolutions have been triggered by innovations in science and technology.

This chapter will highlight the impact that a trifecta of tech-driven exponential thinking, design thinking methodology and an abundance mindset can have on dominating the global business ecosystem.

As a society, we have embarked on the industrial revolution journey, which led us from mechanisation, steam and water power, mass production, electricity, automation, electronic and IT systems all the way to the current cyber physical systems defining the fourth industrial revolution. Given the rapid pace of scientific and technological advances we have witnessed over the past few years, experts estimate that we are likely on the cusp of the fifth industrial revolution.

The latest pandemic has accelerated the adoption of frontier technologies, as well as increased emphasis towards enterprise-adoption of existing technologies.

At the same time, we have witnessed an unprecedented volume of investments in disruptive technologies that are poised to recalibrate, reshape and reconfigure the way we live, work, educate and entertain ourselves currently and future generations.

Numerous international advocacy groups have also increased awareness and demanded a heightened ESG focus in the business arena.

Digital & business transformation & technology trends

Prior to the onset of the latest global pandemic, experts were already predicting an exponential adoption of digital technologies and were encouraging businesses across all industries to engage in the digital transformation journey. With the dramatic worldwide economic and workforce changes we have been experiencing as a consequence of the global pandemic, the predicted time line has markedly accelerated and it has now become an imperative for companies to start or accelerate their digital transformation process. It is now considered critical in order for them to remain viable and/or retain their competitive advantage in a highly disrupted, digital and virtualised environment.

Even during favourable economic times, the road to a successful 'digital transformation' was filled with hurdles and challenges, requiring a comprehensive strategy and disciplined deployment. Given the financial pressures and disruption in business operations due to the pandemic, it is now even more difficult for companies to design, deploy and complete all the stages of digital transformation. To start the journey, these organisations or businesses would need to complete a careful environmental risk analysis to understand what has changed in their value stream, what new stakeholders have emerged and what new forces have disruptive potential.

Afterwards, they would need to understand what has changed in their customer base. Have they lost customer loyalty, have they gained any new customers or is there an opportunity to enter new markets? Additionally, they would have to re-evaluate support from their boards or investors, and if needed, be prepared to pivot or realign the business model.

After these domains have been addressed, they would need to plan a digital strategy that is harmonised with their general enterprise strategy. Additionally, they would have to carefully select and build a digital portfolio that will ensure their ROI and long-term sustainability.

There are several methods to accomplish this, however, the application of design thinking principles seems uniquely suited for a volatile and complex post-pandemic ecosystem due to its agile and human-centred approach.

There are seven core design thinking stages: empathy, definition, ideation, prototyping, selection, implementation and feedback. It allows for increased speed of implementation, improved user satisfaction and cost savings. So, what would a design-thinking powered digital transformation playbook look like?

- Change the culture by shifting to a human-centred mindset, encourage creative confidence in all employees and the leadership team, express empathy for all stakeholders and embrace uncertainty.

- Complete an honest risk and voice-of-the-customer analysis to create an environmental resilience map.
- Encourage all employees to brainstorm, ideate and submit their proposals in order to create a viable ideas funnel.
- Design, build and test a minimum viable live prototype or pilot and schedule playback sessions within the organisation and with key stakeholders to receive valuable feedback.
- Throughout this process it would be essential to maintain transparency and open communication with all employees as that will facilitate engagement, acceptance and successful deployment.

Converging technologies

Over the past decade, we have witnessed an increased adoption of emerging technologies, as well as convergence to augment and amplify their benefits across industries.

The latest pandemic has been a massive catalyst for the digital era. Novel technologies are major drivers of change as they shape our society and economy at maximum velocity. Blending of the boundaries between physical and digital will likely continue with the increased adoption and rapid deployment of these novel technologies. Some of these, such as 5G, IoT, AI, Blockchain and quantum computing have a major disruptive potential globally.

Business leaders are faced with deploying 5G networks, IoT, next-generation computing, next-generation genomic sequencing, nanotechnology, telehealth, artificial intelligence, ledger technologies, AR, VR, XR, holograms, 3D printing, and more recently, quantum technology and human-computer interfaces.

Digital twins

As a [1]Deloitte report highlighted recently, digital twins are designed and deployed to enable virtual collaboration, absorb and process big data, as well as assist us with managing the physical world in a more efficient and safe manner.

There are several industries that have shown significant advancements in using digital twin capabilities, such as automotive, aircraft, energy, urban planning and health care, to name a few. The pandemic impact and disruption caused to the global economy have only accelerated the pace and adoption of digital twins' development globally. Therefore, it is expected that the digital twins' market will reach $48.2 billion by 2026 at a CAGR of 58%. While currently the North American market owns the largest share, it is expected that the APAC market will experience the fastest growth over the next few years.

Per Gartner, a digital twin is a digital representation of a real-world entity or system. The implementation of a digital twin is an encapsulated software object or model that mirrors a unique physical object, process, organisation, person or other abstraction.

The design and deployment of digital twins is complex and intimately connected to other digital technologies such as cloud computing, AI, IoT, 5G networks, blockchain, and virtual, augmented or mixed reality. It is expected that the rate of adoption of all these technologies will have a profound influence on the digital twin industry. Digital twins have dominated all industries, however, experts agree that product and process digital twin types will be on the rise over the next few years.

The benefits we can reap as a society by deploying these digital, highly versatile avatars are vast as they can optimise efficiency,

---

1) www2.deloitte.com/be/en/pages/technology-media-and-telecommunications/articles/digital-twins.html

reduce long-term costs, enhance quality and further our research capabilities.

Metaverse and omniverse

We have witnessed a race by major technology companies to launch new platforms that signal the beginning of a new phase in the digital era: the metaverse and omniverse era.

Those who perhaps believed AI, Blockchain or quantum would be the dominant force of the next industrial revolution are now likely wondering if the metaverse or the omniverse will play that key role. From a futurist's perspective, this is an exciting and long-awaited leap into immersive, multi-sensory and converging technology experiences, however, we must also ask ourselves how will both poorly understood immersive digital ecosystems impact our society and culture? From a digital ethicist's perspective, one can expect significant concerns about how these will impact moral values and the ability to uphold ethical principles.

Global experts were already warning about the profound and transformative socio-cultural impact of quantum, AI, Blockchain, 6G, brain-computer interfaces and other emerging technologies, as well as the need to prevent ethical violations. Now their concerns will be heightened, and key stakeholders are faced with an even more complex metaverse- and omniverse-fuelled digital ethics conundrum.

Before discussing the ethical dilemmas related to large-scale deployments of the metaverse and omniverse, we must first understand how they are defined. As highlighted in a recent technical paper published by [2]Huansheng Ning and colleagues from Cornell University, the metaverse is a new type of internet application and social form that integrates a variety of new technologies.

---
2) arxiv-export-lb.library.cornell.edu/abs/2111.09673

The authors highlight its characteristics which are a symbiotic convergence of established technologies, emerging technologies, social media platform functionality and 'hyper-spatial-temporality'. There is a vacuum of scientific papers on technical or ethical aspects related to the omniverse, however, according to industry leaders, promoting various applications such as Nvidia, it is a trademarked term and represents 'a scalable, multi-GPU real-time reference development platform for 3D simulation and design collaboration, and based on Pixar's Universal Scene Description and NVIDIA RTX technology'.

Some of the key ethical concerns that ethicists are already envisioning for both the metaverse and omniverse are related to consumer trust and rights: 'Misuse or unauthorised use of metaverse- or omniverse-generated data, as well as extreme vulnerability to cyber attacks.' Would the metaverse and omniverse deployments pass a basic ethics checklist?

More than likely not.

It would be difficult to argue that they meet the beneficence criteria, and while some might argue that the intent is clearly to promote innovation and societal progress, they certainly increase the potential for malicious use. Given the multiple breaches published and the stats on cybersecurity that continue to show exponential increases in cyber attacks for major companies, one would be concerned that they both would fail the strictest criteria for confidentiality and integrity.

While we do not have any proof yet regarding their ability or inability to uphold the principles of fidelity, integrity and autonomy, we can certainly extrapolate from past deployments of other emerging technologies that were significantly less sophisticated. That methodology would sadly lead us to expect them both to fail.

If the technology companies that seem to be racing to achieve metaverse or omniverse supremacy would consider state-of-the-art ethics to be a competitive advantage, we might have a pleasant surprise for once in our history and learn valuable insights from our past mistakes. Few companies have understood the need to be proactive and invest up-front in complex digital ethics and data governance programs.

To mitigate the potential negative consequences induced by the metaverse and omniverse, we must advocate for the design and deployment of proactive digital ethics, proactive cyber-defence programs and creating a culture of digital ethics and cyber awareness. Furthermore, these would need to be integrated and harmonised with other enterprise compliance programs to prevent ethical breaches.

While regulatory and legal experts are still trying to bridge the gap in frameworks that can address emerging technologies such as Blockchain, AI or next-generation computing, they must now face an even larger challenge as the metaverse and omniverse are trespassing multiple industry boundaries, while posing unique, novel ethical challenges.

So, who are the key stakeholders that can engage in a global metaverse and omniverse data governance and ethics program? Governments, academia, the private sector and not-for-profit organisations would all have to collaborate to be successful. In addition to legal and regulatory updates, developing international standards, implementing key ethical performance indicators as well as embracing societal expectations of diversity and inclusion will be paramount.

First, we would have to establish the ethical design philosophy and desired outcomes for a society fully immersed in the metaverse and omniverse. Second, we would aim to create a robust ethics architecture that would ensure adequate data governance and address identity management, privacy, security, ownership challenges, etc. Third would be the development of a customised ethical framework for various industries or domains. This framework would include the impact on society, the environment, long-term sustainability, education and emphasis on ESGs.

Pessimists will likely envision the worst possible outcomes with a negative impact on education, arts, culture, social interaction, etc. Optimists will hope that companies leading the charge in deploying the metaverse and omniverse would be ethically and purpose driven, with a vision and mission that aim to deliver 'ethical, transparent' services or even to facilitate the attainment of UN SDGs.

Smart cities and communities

We are currently witnessing what is called by some international experts 'the smart city revolution'. The COVID-19 pandemic induced global crisis and has only accentuated pre-existent economic and social challenges. These unprecedented times call for innovative solutions and a revised approach to manage this volatile post-pandemic global business environment and for us to adapt to major emerging technology mega trends.

As reported by the World Economic Forum, cities find themselves at the centre of the global crisis and must rethink, recalibrate and rebuild the economy by designing cities that are more 'livable, sustainable, resilient and affordable'. The G20 Global Smart Cities Alliance unites various stakeholders around a shared goal of responsible and ethical technology deployment for smart cities.

The OECD white paper on [3]'Smart Cities and Inclusive Growth' focused on the powerful role technology can play in

---

3) smart-cities-marketplace.ec.europa.eu/news-and-events/news/2020/new-oecd-policy-paper-smart-cities-and-inclusive-growth#:~:text=Going%20forward%2C%20the%20OECD%20Programme,from%20the%20COVID%2D19%20crisis

relying on lifesaving information, supporting the shift towards remote work, ensuring remote service delivery and bridge social isolation. As highlighted by the World Bank session on 'Pathways to Sustainable Urban Development', by 2050, 80% of the global population is expected to live in urban environments, and cities must strengthen their commitment to design and deploy sustainable urban infrastructures.

A 2020 Barclays Investment Bank report pointed out the massive business potential heralded by smart cities as there is a potential for them to generate $20 trillion in economic benefits by 2026. The main infrastructure investment opportunities identified are technology enablement, building and construction, energy, water and waste management. In a Deloitte Smart Cities of the Future report, smart cities are defined as urban centres that not only leverage technology to improve their own operations but also connect with citizens, businesses and non-profits in novel ways.

To be successful, all key stakeholders of the global urban development ecosystem need to be open to novel funding sources, novel business models, novel implementation strategies and use design thinking for planning the smart cities of the future.

When deploying the seven principles of design thinking across all domains that define smart cities, we can more accurately capture the pain points of all stakeholders, benefit from the enhanced creativity generated when fostering an innovation mindset and adapt to a highly dynamic economic landscape. Over the past decades, design thinking has been mostly associated with innovation, however, it has gradually transcended into other business domains and is now more widely adopted as a mindset that embodies empathy, iterative processes, creative confidence, comfort with experimentation and embracing ambiguity or potential failure.

By designing and deploying human-centric cities and a

continuous improvement mindset we can ensure long-term sustainability for the smart cities we develop. Specifically, the first principle of empathy is a crucial step that aims to understand the needs of all customers in a smart city and ensure that we build them to be inclusive to all types of populations such as children, elderly and disabled. Adequately defining the exact needs of each of the stakeholders and customers during the second step in the design thinking process is the most complex, yet, an essential driver of success. Principles three, four and five, that encompass researching, indexing and prototyping, will require inter- and cross-disciplinary collaboration, as the current global landscape is marked by a convergence of technologies and blurring of traditional industry boundaries.

The sixth principle of selecting and implementing is equally important if we aim to ensure adaptability, agility, inclusion and long-term sustainability of our smart cities. One of the major reasons for failure is lack of desire or diligence towards the seventh principle of design thinking which is learning. Building smart cities is not a one-time project. We must be ready to engage in a culture of ongoing quality improvement, ongoing transformation and micro-innovation if we wish these smart cities to be future ready.

There are several challenges we can encounter when using design thinking methodology. There is a danger of misalignment with other strategic priorities, potential to underestimate financial and legal risks, as well as a tendency to only involve specific stakeholders due to a bias problem towards creative methodologies. Perhaps one of the most significant challenges is attempting and succeeding in harmonising design thinking methodology with legislative guidelines and regulatory policies.

Smart cities are one of the solutions that can address the digital divide by creating a state-of-the-art technology infrastructure. By increasing smartphone adoption, optimising access to the internet or higher internet speed, offering 5G or 6G broadband, enabling cloud markets and data centres, securing satellite-powered data communications or facilitating ecommerce via neo banking solutions, people can stimulate the digital economy and improve the overall quality of life for citizens.

The global smart cities market is estimated to surpass $2.5 trillion by 2025, according to [4]PwC. As reported by several organisations, cities must rebuild new digital urban ecosystems that are viable in the post-pandemic economy and the next industrial revolution. The design of these smart cities built for smart citizens of the digital era must focus on the quality of life, economic competitiveness and sustainability as highlighted in a recent report by Deloitte.

Global business ecosystem drivers: a trifecta

In addition to scientific advances, it is essential for business leaders to embrace exponential thinking, design thinking and an abundance mindset.

Defined as being able to conceive things that can compound exponential thinking certainly explains some of the massive societal and business ecosystem advances we have observed in this digital era. This type of thinking style has been promoted by leaders of the innovation ecosystem Ray Kurzweil and X Prize Foundation chairman and CEO Peter Diamandis.

The abundance mindset concept stems from Stephen Covey's acclaimed book, *The Seven Habits of Highly Effective People,* and has been foundational in countless entrepreneurship incubators and accelerators worldwide due to its massive success.

While design thinking methodology was originally deployed

---

4) pwc.com/us/en/industries/industrial-products/capital-projects-infrastructure/smart-cities.html

by pioneers like Tim Brown and Roger Martin to counteract a rigid corporate mindset, it has evolved and expanded and is now emblematic of being able to dynamically adapt to consumer's needs and the environment to gain competitive advantage and drive business growth.

By using a combined approach of design thinking in conjunction with exponential thinking and an abundance mindset, we can markedly amplify our success in building future-ready business ecosystems. By leveraging all the benefits each of these three methodologies can offer, we have a higher potential of building inclusive and sustainable global business ecosystems.

Adopting an abundance mindset can also facilitate global solutions and assist us in overcoming traditional geographic barriers and industry silos. By embracing and engaging in a global abundance movement when designing, developing, deploying and maintaining novel business ecosystems, we can ensure adaptability and maintain a competitive advantage in a high-risk, highly volatile global economic environment.

Challenges: legal, regulatory & compliance

Legal and regulatory compliance frameworks have always lagged behind scientific and technology adoptions. To be successful we must engage in dynamic global collaborative efforts with key stakeholders and decision-makers that will aim to solve major regional- and country-specific differences that are currently perceived or real barriers to a global business ecosystem.

Cost and funding instruments

There continues to be a major financial and digital divide in the global business ecosystem. Developing novel programs and support systems that can ease access to funding and improve financial inclusion and digital literacy will be essential for a flourishing and sustainable business ecosystem. Novel funding mechanisms must be developed that offer small- and medium-sized businesses an equal chance to play a key role in the global business ecosystem.

Ethics & cyber attacks

Although ethics and moral values have been in existence for centuries, the digital era and rapid large-scale adoption of emerging technologies, such as Blockchain, are posing novel digital ethics challenges that need to be addressed from a philosophical, legal and self-sovereignty perspective.

Digital data ownership, digital identity and digital privacy are the foundational elements, and blatant violations keep making headlines frequently. At a more advanced level, the fusion of AI, Blockchain and digital assets or crypto assets with other financial instruments and technologies creates the need for a complex digital ethics program. Given the IoT trend and scaling of 5G networks, we are witnessing a state-of-the-art cyber ethics program that must be on every leader's agenda.

It has become evident that the exponential adoption of converging technologies and ongoing innovative forces will require a sustainable digital ethics culture to prevent potential violations of trust, integrity, digital privacy, digital ownership, etc. Business leaders should be appropriately concerned about general ethical issues, as well as those unique to the business ecosystem. Reactive or mitigation approaches are not an optimal solution, and one would hope that ethical leadership in the digital era will be marked by state-of-the-art strategic planning and careful tactical deployments. A great quote that illustrates the importance of creating a robust ethical governance infrastructure within the organisation was by Alfred Einstein who stated, 'Relativity applies to physics, not to ethics.'

However, the digital era also poses new challenges that need to be overcome. In addition to the legal, regulatory and socioeconomic factors that exist in many regional markets, key stakeholders will also have to address cybersecurity, data stewardship and ownership, interoperability and cross-border portability, as well as prove their ESG-consciousness with reliable metrics. Business leaders will also have to adapt to this new, highly volatile, higher risk, hyper-connected and hyper-virtualised economic landscape by developing new business models that can meet the new demands of the digital era.

Opportunities & ethical leadership

Leaders that wish to succeed in this highly virtualised, digitalised and hyper-connected environment will be required to display a complex armamentarium of novel skills, such as digital literacy and fluency, global citizenship, design thinking and mastery of applied ethics. Within the ethics realm, there are several domains to consider in a state-of-the-art business strategic road map: digital ethics, cyber ethics, business ethics and leadership ethics.

Digital ethics addresses behaviours related to digital mediums, norms related to the use of digital tools, autonomy and ownership of online data, etc. Business ethics include governance, social and fiduciary responsibilities, as well as discrimination, fraud, abuse or bribery. Ethical business leaders are expected to display a high regard for moral values such as honesty, fairness and respect for others. It will be important for leaders in this digital era to dedicate resources to all of those and to embed them into the fabric of their enterprise strategy.

By striving to demonstrate ethical leadership in this digital era, business leaders can greatly contribute to the development of a global culture of digital ethics. As Heraclitus stated: 'Character is destiny.' So, what are the key character traits of an ethical digital era leader? As a recent article in Forbes Business Council highlighted, leading by example and cultivating external awareness are crucial, particularly during times of crisis or disruption. Additionally, an ethical leader shows empathy, puts his team first and displays a high degree of moral integrity.

Inclusive & diverse leadership

As author Bianca Weber eloquently described in a recently published article, diverse leadership can be defined as an approach to empower digital innovation, which is a key driver of digital and business transformation. This process demands human transformation to complement business transformation to achieve long-term sustainability. Changing the culture, fostering an inclusive mindset and guaranteeing diversity are challenging yet foundational elements in building a legacy and require inclusive digital ethics leadership. Our society needs to undergo disruptive and transformative changes to adapt to exponential technological advances in the educational, professional, cultural and governance fields.

The digital era holds great potential for increased inclusion, reduction or even closure of the gender leadership gap in all industries. Diverse leadership is a moral imperative for our society, and we must collaborate to trigger a paradigm change and highlight the benefits of leveraging women's potential in the social, digital and business transformation arenas.

Greater efforts are needed to fill an 'ethical vacuum' brought to light by the emerging technologies' revolution. We must dedicate more resources and have a heightened focus on both ethical and data governance aspects in digital innovation. Identifying novel approaches to answer how diverse leadership can contribute towards avoiding gender bias, optimising inclusion and further improving crucial digital ethics aspects in data-driven technologies are essential for long-term success.

Building a culture of digital ethics & cyber resilience

For centuries, ethical principles have been foundational in our society. After decades of marginalisation, we are currently witnessing a digital renaissance within the scientific and business community due to the complex ethical issues we are facing in this digital era. Business leaders can shape the future by fostering a culture of digital ethics and contributing to the development of a global ethics framework. This will require a strong emphasis on educating and training the workforce, as well as creating an environment where citizens and employees are part of a robust digital ethics governance ecosystem.

Reactive cyber defense systems have proven ineffective, and it has become increasingly clear that business leaders who wish to maintain or gain competitive advantage, as well as restore trust, must build a robust, sustainable cyber resilience program. This would also require increased dedication to prevention, more frequent vulnerability testing to cyber attacks, changing budget allocations, as well as education and training of the workforce.

Both cultures require a strong emphasis on ongoing quality improvement and integration of human-computer feedback loops.

New business models

Looking beyond the impact of the pandemic-related global policy reforms and governmental stimulus packages, business leaders must focus on new funding instruments, novel strategic partnerships and upskilling or reskilling the workforce. These can only be achieved by designing and deploying novel business models that are dynamic, as well as adaptable to a highly globalised, volatile economic environment. Traditional business models will no longer suffice when aiming to design future-ready sustainable business ecosystems for the next generations.

There are several innovative business models that can be deployed to gain competitive advantage or avoid being disrupted in this digital era, and these include data-driven, digital-economy-driven, partnership-driven, purpose-driven or sustainability-driven business models. Each one of these offers unique benefits, and I believe they should be considered when planning state-of-the-art smart city deployments to attain long-term success.

Through global collaboration among all key stakeholders such as governments, not-for-profit agencies, policymakers, compliance experts, academicians and business leaders, people can further their research into what business models will be most suitable and afford the highest agility to pivot when faced by unexpected new socioeconomic crises they might encounter as a society.

Perhaps abundance-driven or global-ecosystem-driven mindsets for key global indicators could lead to viable solutions when drafting the global smart city business canvas. A carefully crafted balance among resources utilised, environmental impact, social benefits and risks and economic benefit will be essential for future generations of smart citizens to thrive in smart urban ecosystems. Engaging in alternative funding models, revenue sharing initiatives, leveraging multi-city deployments and public-private partnerships must be at the core of their efforts.

While crafting new business models is crucial, it is also their duty to educate, train and employ the smart digital citizens that will live, learn and work in the smart cities of the digital era. According to one report, it is expected that 70% of the human population will live in urban areas by 2050. Only by adopting a human-centric approach, grounded in the principles of design thinking, can you be successful in building the digital era metropolis that embeds information and communication technologies into its DNA.

Alignment with United Nations Sustainable Development Goals & human rights

Perhaps one of the most important changes business leaders are facing is a heightened demand to align their enterprise strategy with the United Nations 2030 SDG agenda and engage in proactive programs that respect human rights. This will require a profound change in their approach and mindset.

Experts are noticing a higher emphasis on impact investing and increased advocacy efforts to encourage or stimulate the attainment of the United Nations Sustainable Development Agenda 2030, as well as a profound disruption in the global workforce due to high degrees of automation, digitisation and hybrid intelligence-enablement.

Current and future generations of global digital citizens expect purpose-driven organisations. Consumer trust in the web 3.0 era is defined by a decentralised, trustless, permissionless, ubiquitous, hyper-connected architecture and will be heavily human-centric facilitating adherence to individual digital citizens' rights.

Dominate through technology

To dominate the business ecosystem, business leaders must enhance their portfolio of professional expertise with other crucial skills such as digital ethics fluency, exponential thinking, abundance mindset and embrace a purposeful, inclusive leadership style. The shift towards web 3.0 will require adaptation to new business models, new financial instruments and transition from a finance-driven global ecosystem to a human-centric business ecosystem.

Lastly, it is this author's opinion that business leaders must be lifelong learners to keep pace with a continuously evolving tech-driven business ecosystem.

DR INGRID VASILIU-FELTES

Ingrid is a health care executive, futurist and globalist who is highly dedicated to digital and ethics advocacy. She is a Forbes Business Council member, digital strategist, passionate educator and entrepreneurship ecosystem builder, known as an expert speaker, board advisor and consultant.

Throughout her career she has received several awards for excellence in research, teaching or leadership. She is the recipient of numerous awards, most notably: WBAF World Excellence Award – Social Entrepreneurship 2021, Top 25 Quantum Technology Leader, Top 20 Global Leaders in Digital Twins Technologies, Top 50 Global Leaders in Health Tech, Top 50 Global Ecosystem Leaders, Top 100 Visionary in Education Award 2021, Top 100 Global Women in Leadership Award 2021, Top 100 World Women

Vision Award 2021 – Innovation & Tech, Top 150 Women in Business To Follow, Top 100 Women in Social Enterprise 2021 (nominee), Top 50 Global Thinkers (nominee), Nations of Women Change Makers Award (finalist), Top 100 Healthcare Leader 2020 Award, Top 100 Finance Leader 2020 Award and Top 100 Women in Crypto 2020. Additionally, she serves as an expert advisor to the EU Blockchain Observatory and Forum and was appointed to the board of advisors for several organisations.

During her academic tenure she taught several courses within the medical school as well as the combined MD/PhD and MD/MPH programs. Throughout her career, Dr Vasiliu-Feltes held several leadership positions and is a member of numerous prestigious professional organisations. She holds several certifications, such as Bioethics from Harvard, Artificial Intelligence and Business Strategy from MIT Sloan, Blockchain Technology and Business Innovation from MIT Sloan, Finance from Harvard Business School, Negotiation from Harvard Law School, Innovation and Entrepreneurship from Stanford Graduate School of Business, Certified Professional in Healthcare Risk Management, Fellow of the American College of Healthcare Executives, Patient Safety Officer by the International Board Federation of Safety Managers, Master Black Belt in Lean and Six Sigma Management, Professional in Healthcare Quality by the National Association of Healthcare Quality, Manager for Quality and Organizational Excellence, by the American Society for Quality, and Certified Risk Management Professional by the American Society for Healthcare Risk Management.

Dr Vasiliu-Feltes is CEO of Softhread Inc., the founder and CEO of the Institute for Science, Entrepreneurship and Investments, founder and CEO of Revexpo Consulting and currently serving as a country director for WBAF USA, senator of WBAF, faculty member of the WBAF Business School – Division of Entrepreneurship, and teaching the Executive MBA Business Technology Course at the UM Business School. She is also acting as the chief innovation officer for Government Blockchain Association. Most recently she served as president of Detect Genomix, chief quality and safety officer and innovation officer for Mednax, chief quality and safety officer and chief of compliance for the University of Miami UHealth System.

Additionally, Dr Vasiliu-Feltes is an honorary advisory board member of several companies, entrepreneurship incubators or accelerators, as well as an editorial board member for several international publications, an author, keynote speaker and TV/media partner.

HOW DOES YOUR BRAIN HEALTH AFFECT YOUR BUSINESS SUCCESS?

Dr Isabel Bertran-Hunsinger MD

There is a wall right in front of all of us. And on that wall are the words mental illness, and in particular, anxiety and depression. With anxiety and depression comes shame – like you're crazy, you're bad or you've done something wrong. The latest medical research shows that it's not a mental illness problem that's going on, it's a brain health issue. Unfortunately, many of us are not taught how to take care of our brain health.

The brain is a very important organ. If you break a bone, you go get an X-ray. It shows that it's broken, and you get a cast. No-one is saying you're crazy or you're bad, or you should feel ashamed for a broken bone. As a matter of fact, everybody wants to write their name on your cast or say something funny on your profile. The point is your bone is an organ.

Similarly, if you're having chest pain, you call the ambulance, they take you to the emergency department and you are diagnosed with a heart attack. They take care of you, and you are discharged home. Two weeks later, you're having a meal with your friends, you tell them what happened. No-one is saying you're a bad person, you're crazy or they don't make you feel ashamed. They feel sympathetic. They say, 'Wow, how are you doing? How are you feeling?' Because your heart is an organ too.

The same can be said for the brain. The brain is an organ, and we need to understand that we've got to take very, very good care of our brain. You see, a healthy brain leads to a happy mind. And when we have a happy mind, we're able to deal with life and all that comes with it. That's why I want to talk to you about your sleep. Your sleep is an important ingredient for optimal brain health. Wouldn't you want to increase all your chances of having a successful business? Then let's begin with your sleep.

Learning to sleep well is part of maintaining a healthy brain. I was taught how *not* to sleep in my medical training and in life. I could sleep only two to three hours per night and continue working. That made me very, very sick.

Here's a little bit about my story. I've been a medical doctor since 1991. In 2013, I decided that I wanted to help people outside of my practice. I was going to go out into the internet world and into the 'cloud'.

So, we started Doctor On A Mission. I say 'we' because my husband, Chef Michael, who's the certified nutritional expert at Doctor On A Mission, actually started this campaign. And Doctor On A Mission's goal was to prevent and reverse disease and give people hope in the process. Because a lot of the chronic disease that we're seeing out there is preventable and reversible.

One year later, in 2014, I found myself overwhelmed with fear. I was listening to the inner critic saying, *You can't do this. You don't know how to do this.* As a by-product of this project,

I became fearful and overwhelmed, and I didn't sleep. This is a regular pattern of mine. Unfortunately, I went through seventeen straight nights of only sleeping two to three hours per night. By the end of those seventeen days, I tried to take my life twice in three days. By the grace of God those plans were interrupted.

My husband took me to the doctor, and she immediately referred me to the psychiatrist. The psychiatrist (who was a lovely guy), immediately put me on medication, and I remember him saying, 'Isabel, you're going to be on this antidepressant and sleeping tablet for the rest of your life.' At that point, I had completely surrendered. I was going to do whatever I needed to do to get well.

Honestly, I just wanted to get a good night's sleep. I agreed to the medication, however, deep down in my soul, I said, *Hmm, we'll see about that. We'll see if I'll be on this medicine FOR THE REST OF MY LIFE.* After some time, when I was getting decent sleep, my soul woke up and said, *Hey, Isabel, you are in the health care system with a mental illness. Now you are experiencing what your patients were experiencing,* and I did not like it. This led me to go on a journey that lasted five years. I was determined to get out of that place. I knew, as a functional medical doctor who is trained to uncover the root causes of one's illness, I had to begin my journey to uncover my own causes of anxiety and depression.

I learned what is not taught in mainstream medicine: how to reverse anxiety and depression. There's a saying in functional medicine, if you're stepping on a thumbtack, you don't give pain medicine for the foot pain, you actually want to get your foot off the tack. I went on a journey to find out all the causes of my anxiety and depression, and the research was amazing.

What was revealed, I can never unlearn

Now, I'm off medication safely. I'm calm, and I know how to turn up the microphone to my inner cheerleader. I'm on a mission to help women overcome anxiety and depression because as a medical doctor who struggled and almost died from it, I can honestly say I know that place and I also know the way out of it. There's this saying I heard, 'Where there is pain in life, there is a lesson and a blessing.' There were many lessons regarding all the things that can cause anxiety and depression in women that aren't being taught to us in our medical training. I feel so blessed because I'm here, alive, and I get to live life and share it with my beautiful family and friends. Most importantly, I help my women and my sisterhood in ways other doctors cannot. Essentially, I had to unlearn what I learned in medical training about mental illness and mental health. As a result, I became an expert in sleep.

For a moment, let's pretend that you and I are sitting face to face, having a chat. I have a cup of coffee in my hand, and you have a cup of your favourite beverage. Let's ask the question, 'Is sleep really that important to you?'

Well, I've had patients that come to me and say, 'I only sleep four to five hours a night and that's normal. That's just the way it is.' And as a doctor trained only to sleep three hours for a thirty-six-hour shift, I know that is mentally damaging.

You see, sleep dictates how much we eat. If we don't sleep, we have decreased energy. And that causes us to have an increased consumption of food just to get our energy levels up. We are craving energy, so we consume higher levels of carbohydrates, which, if too much, is actually quite unhealthy.

Sleep dictates how fast our metabolism runs. If we get minimal sleep, it decreases our metabolism, and we gain weight. Who wants to gain weight if you're not trying to? Sleep dictates how fat or thin we get. I am not saying body size is the issue here, it's about health and wellbeing in our bodies. Decreased sleep increases the stress response called cortisol, which increases your blood sugar, which causes an increase in insulin and ultimately causes fat storage. Sleep also dictates how well we fight off infections and how creative and insightful we are. Not getting enough sleep can cause brain fog.

Sleep dictates how well we cope with stress. Good sleep leads to good coping skills, and conversely, bad sleep leads to bad coping skills. Sleep dictates how well we can organise and store memories in a part of the brain called the hippocampus. Sleep also influences our genes. In 2013, scientists in England found that one week of sleep deprivation affected 711 genes. These genes were involved in the stress response, inflammation, immunity and metabolism. You see, one choice of deciding that you don't need that much sleep can affect seven-hundred-plus outcomes in your life. That's why I stress the importance of sleep. My prescription for adequate sleep, from research and from my experience, is seven to nine hours per night.

So, what are the side effects of chronic poor sleep? Confusion, memory loss, poor focus, you get sicker faster, an increased risk of heart disease like heart attacks, obesity, depression, anxiety and type two diabetes. Sleep is important to prevent and cure depression and anxiety.

What about sleeping tablets? Did you know that they negatively affect our brain? Sleeping tablets may seem to work at first, but the long-term effect is on our memory. Let's just look at the equation. Decreased sleep leads to anxiety and depression, which increases our risk of Alzheimer's disease. I'll break that down. Decreased sleep leads to anxiety and depression. The reason is because most of the time you go to the doctor, they put you on an antidepressant and an antianxiety medication, which is a sleeping tablet to help you get your sleep. Well, the problem with that is most of these medications are anticholinergics.

And the reason that's important is because acetylcholine is food for your brain. It helps us increase our memory and learning. An anticholinergic really is an anti-acetylcholine medication. It blocks the action of acetylcholine in the brain. Now, there are two groups of sleeping medications. One is benzodiazepines – often called downers – and then non-benzodiazepines.

Let's start with the benzodiazepines. The latest research shows that benzodiazepines, if taken for three to six months, increase your risk of developing Alzheimer's by 32%. If taken for more than six months, it increases your risk of developing Alzheimer's by 84%. If taken for more than a year, memory loss can continue beyond stopping the benzodiazepine for up to 3.5 years! So, benzodiazepines can increase your risk of Alzheimer's disease.

The next category are non-benzodiazepines. Now, in the non-benzodiazepine group are another two categories: non-benzodiazepines and antihistamines. Antihistamines decrease acetylcholine absorption into your brain and hence decrease memory and learning just like benzodiazepines. Why? Because most of them are anticholinergics, as we discussed above, and they increase your risk of Alzheimer's too. The antihistamines are Benadryl, Tylenol PM, Advil PM and promethazine. In the non-benzodiazepines group are some well-known names such as Imovane, Ambien, Lunesta and Sonata.

Another sleep drug that a lot of us take is alcohol. The problem with alcohol is, yes, it does get us to sleep, but it disrupts our REM sleep (deep sleep) which is when we dream, and we need to be able to dream.

Let's talk about supplements and medications that can induce better sleep without the negative effects. I'd like for you to try one at a time and journal the effects. Layer them as needed and tweak until you find a combination that is right for you. Remember you are a unique individual, and you need your own personalised and specialised combination for the unrepeatable miracle that you are.

Magnesium threonate

This gets into your brain better, increases cognition, which includes your ability to think and understand, and it also induces sleep. The recommendation is 2g of magnesium threonate one hour before bed. Keep in mind that it only has 144mg of magnesium.

Other benefits include the reduction of muscle tension, spasms or cramps, constipation, headaches, heart palpitations, PMS symptoms, nervousness and irritability. Disclaimer: Ask your GP or your doctor if you have heart disease or kidney stones before you take magnesium.

Ashwagandha

Ashwagandha is an adaptogenic herb used in Ayurvedic medicine. The benefits are it improves sleep quality and brain health, decreases fatigue, improves mood, helps with stress management, reduces stress response and improves mental focus. The recommendation is 500mg one to two times a day. Range is 2-4g per day.

Bacopa monnieri

This is also an Ayurvedic adaptogenic herb, which increases the acetylcholine. And as you learned above, that increases our memory and learning because it's food for the brain. It's good for those having trouble sleeping due to stress. Now, it may cause increased energy, so start low with, say, 100mg several hours before bed, and journal how you feel.

5-HTP

This improves sleep and mood. Tryptophan, which is found in milk, eggs, poultry and fish becomes 5-HTP, which then gets converted into serotonin and melatonin. The recommendation for this is 100-200mg in the morning on an empty stomach. Disclaimer, if you are on an SSRI, which is a selective serotonin reuptake inhibitor, you do not want to take 5-HTP because it increases serotonin. And if you've got too much serotonin in your brain, you can experience serotonin syndrome, which is expressed in you as shivering, diarrhoea, rigidity, fever and seizures. So no 5-HTP if you are on an SSRI.

Bioidentical hormone

Bioidentical hormone replacement, body identical hormone replacement or natural hormone replacement. The importance of this differentiation is that these hormones best resemble the hormones your body makes. The first I recommend from my research findings, and the second from personal experience is progesterone and micronized progesterone.

This restores disturbed sleep. Pretty much around the world, you can get it as Utrogestan or Prometrium. The dose is between 100-200mg per night, taken about half an hour before bed. I have to say, I wish I would have known about this in my thirties and forties when I suffered dreadfully with PMS, because it helps with mood swings and anxiety.

The next bioidentical hormone is estradiol. This improves sleep by helping you with nervousness. The prescription is dependent on your specific needs. You will need to talk to your doctor about this. The research shows that two-thirds of people with Alzheimer's are women, and up to 38% of those could have been prevented with the use of bioidentical hormones in perimenopause and early menopause.

Melatonin

Melatonin is a hormone created by your pineal gland, which is in your brain. As we age, it decreases. The benefit of taking melatonin is it improves sleep via a healthy circadian rhythm. It improves your mitochondria, which are your energy stores in each of your cells, and it improves cognition. The recommendation is 1-2mg an hour before bed.

Magnesium

Magnesium is necessary for up to a hundred biochemical reactions in your body, and especially your brain. Magnesium citrate is recommended if you tend towards constipation, magnesium glycinate if you tend towards having diarrhoea. The recommendation is 200-400mg at night. Keep in mind, if you are using magnesium threonate, which has 144mg of magnesium, then you only want to be doing 200mg of the citrate or the glycinate. Again, another disclaimer, ask your GP if you can use magnesium if you suffer from heart and kidney problems.

Taurine

Taurine is an amino acid, and it is good to take one hour before bed at 500-2,000mg.

Lastly, and wait for it, is laughter

Now, laughter is a very wonderful medication. You don't have to buy it. You can do it right away. You see, your brain does not know the difference between fake laughter or real laughter. And when you laugh for even fifteen seconds straight, it increases the happy hormone called dopamine.

Dopamine tells your brain, *Hey, I'm not stressed anymore*, so it decreases the cortisol, and having high levels of dopamine helps you know in your brain, specifically in your limbic system, that you're safe. It's safe to go to sleep. I love YouTube laughing zebras. Oh my gosh, that will get you going. It's just hilarious.

Here's the magical blueprint for improving sleep patterns according to research. Getting ready for sleep all starts about three hours before going to bed. Importantly, avoid eating anything three hours before bed. The reason for this is it induces autophagy, and autophagy is the body's way of cleaning the house. It allows your body to clean out all the cellular debris so that you sleep better on an empty stomach. No caffeine, no hot chocolate, no green tea and no alcohol because it affects your deep sleep, which is when you get to dream. It is also important to avoid exercise and wear blue-blocking glasses three hours before going to bed.

Blue-blocking glasses block the light from going into the back of your eye which stops the secretion of melatonin. So melatonin can still be secreted by your pineal gland so that you can start getting ready for sleep. But if you're not wearing blue-blocking glasses, then your brain's being told, *Oh, I need to stay up. It's not time to secrete melatonin. I better stop secreting melatonin because it's time to rock and roll, baby.* Essentially, your brain is lit up like the lights in New York City.

One hour before bed, no computer, iPad, iPhone or any electronic device – which, I know, is not as easy as it sounds. No scary movies and no TV. This is a good time to get ready for bed, so you shower, bathe, do your skin care and teeth care. And if you'd like something warm before bed, try warm coconut or almond milk.

At bedtime, turn off the router. This is to decrease the wi-fi in your house, which decreases the electromagnetic frequency, so your house isn't like a transmitting radio station. If you use your phone as an alarm, just put it on aeroplane mode, and that decreases the wi-fi exposure. Remember to put the phone away, but not under your pillow or in the same room.

The best way to sleep is on your side to allow for glymphatic drainage. Your glymphatic system cleans out all the toxins. The latest medical research has shown that we've got a glymphatic system in our brain and when we lay on one side or the other, it helps drain all the debris in our brain, and we wake up fresh. That's a little tricky for people who love to sleep on their stomach, so give yourself time to learn how to do that.

It would be great if all we had to do was just read one chapter in a book to optimise our brain health long-term, right? However, we are humans, and that's not the way life is. There are more areas we need to look at to create a healthy brain long-term.

I love the saying, 'We become our strongest in our weakest place.' Now, this does not mean we become stronger because of our weak place. It does not mean that we may become stronger in the places where we are now weak. Rather, it says we become our strongest version in the place which is now our weakest spot.

Another way to look at it is with the process of welding where you take two pieces of the same metal and apply heat. At first, the joint is weak while you're applying the heat. It's still breakable. However, over time, you focus the applied heat and the join becomes the strongest part. Well, that's the same thing when dealing with anxiety and depression. All you need to do is just learn small, focused tools to help you become strong where you were once weak.

I understand that place. I have been in that place, and it's a dreadful pit. As a professional woman suffering from anxiety and depression, I wish during my darkest days I had read this. That was not the case for me; however, I can be that person for you. I have become an expert in the area of brain health for women through personal experience and research.

You see, it's not a mental illness issue, it's a brain health issue. When we are taught how to take good care of our brain health, then we will experience mental wellbeing. Mental wellbeing enables us to deal with all of life's challenges effectively.

Until then, remain unstoppable and press on.

With love, Dr Isabel MD

References:
1. *Why We Sleep* by Matthew Walker PhD.
2. *The End of Mental Illness* by Daniel Amen MD.
3. *The XX Brain* by Lisa Masconi PhD.

DR ISABEL BERTRAN-HUNSINGER

I'm Cuban-American born in 1959 in Washington DC. Now, I don't tell everyone my birth year – but because you have decided to read this, I thought it best that you get to know who I am from the beginning.

I have been a medical doctor since 1991. The only reason I went into the medical field was because I wanted to help people. I wanted to get to the root of the disease, not just throw a bandage on it. My patients weren't getting any better, they were just existing. My goal is to see people healed.

The decision to become a doctor was planted in my mind when I was five years old. My uncle, Dr Julio Perez, an anaesthesiologist, has this amazing way about him. When he walked in, his smile and his positive attitude would light up the room. He would just make you feel happy, and you would start smiling. At five years of age I decided, and I said to my mom, 'I want to be a doctor just like Tio Julito.'

In 2000, my husband and our two young daughters moved to New Zealand to see what it's like to experience a different culture of the world. Yes, we had never been there or even knew where it was. What a crazy and life-changing decision for our family!

I have been studying functional medicine, which focuses on the root cause of disease and its treatments. As a result of my training I am able to offer a blend of conventional and functional medicine for your best outcome.

My husband, certified culinary nutrition expert, Chef Michael, and I created the brand of Doctor On A Mission, where we prevent and reverse disease and give hope. Our expertise is in preventing and reversing early Alzheimer's, dementia, cognitive decline, anxiety and depression. We have been doing telemedicine since 2015 with our online business of doctoronamission.com which offers online courses, group coaching and one-on-one coaching.

And so, here we are, together. Let's start walking together, and I'll share with you what worked for me and can also work for you. I want to give you hope.

Your friend, Dr Isabel MD

Qualifications:
- University of Colorado, Boulder, USA (pre-med) MCDB – September 1982 – May – 1986.
- University of Colorado Medical School, Denver, USA – September 1987 – May 1991.
- Southern Colorado Family Practice Residency, Pueblo, USA – September 1992 – May 1995.

- Fellow of the Royal New Zealand College of General Practice – 2005 – present.
- Member of the Institute of Functional Medicine, USA - March 2018 – present.
- Dr Dale Bredesen Certified 2.0 Recode Protocol Practitioner – January 2018 – present.

BREAKING THE GLASS CEILING FOR WOMEN OF COLOUR IN MEDICAL LEADERSHIP

Dr M Talat Uppal

Marilyn Loden coined the phrase 'glass ceiling' when speaking as a panelist at a 1978 women's exposition in New York. It is a term that refers to a metaphorical invisible barrier that prevents women and minorities from being promoted to senior positions within an organisation or industry.

This concept was later discussed in a 1986 *Wall Street Journal* article, outlining the corporate hierarchy that prevents women from advancing their careers to higher roles.

When it comes to women of colour representation, the statistics are frankly dismal. Thankfully this is a changing space, albeit slowly. I have spent most of my professional life participating in forums and spaces where hardly anyone looks like me. This only worsened the more senior I became. Countless times I have been in meetings where I have been mostly surrounded by clones of older white men.

Women's health has been a particularly patriarchal space until recently, when the numbers of female obstetric and gynaecological trainees have increased nationally, interestingly to an obvious majority at present. However, the pipeline effect to leadership positions takes time.

Change is in the air though, and my personal experience of providing a streamlined, unique and team-based model of care for women has been a positive one overall. I cannot underestimate how many hoops I have had to jump through to get to this point, but as I say, 'You mostly land on your feet, and if you don't, you fall forward trying!'

My desire was to provide a service for the community that would be holistic and cover a wider breadth of obstetrics and gynaecology. It would aim to match women to the exact skill set that would be ideal to manage their care, particularly if they needed advanced surgical care and planning.

I named this model the 'Women's Health Road', as I felt women are constantly on journeys at different points of their life – while some are trying to have a baby, others desire contraception, some are diagnosed with an ovarian cyst and many require pregnancy and birth-based support.

Further along, they may benefit from menopause management, as well as experience issues with urinary and faecal incontinence and prolapse. These are life-altering conditions that women face during their reproductive and postmenopausal health. Obstetrics is widely assumed to be a happy space, which mostly it is. However, one cannot underestimate the grief of loss of pregnancy for some women and their families.

At times, there are very complex decisions that need to be made regarding continuing the pregnancy versus a termination. Similarly, the breaking of bad news – for example if a malignancy is diagnosed – needs to be done with utmost compassion and empathy.

Although we have learned much during the set-up and rollout of this practice, and are constantly trying to improve our system based on staff and patient feedback, it has been so fulfilling and humbling to be able to serve the community. We have found that we are referred disproportionately to women with a history of previous sexual assault, profuse health anxiety and other mental health issues, in addition to their gynaecological or obstetric needs.

We look after so many women with previous trauma (including birth trauma), and although it may take far longer, it is also extremely rewarding to be able to support them at a time when they may be feeling especially vulnerable. It can be quite confronting to need gynaecological procedures and we created the physical space, decor and layout at Women's Health Road to reflect calm. The music that is played in the background is selected deliberately to help minimise anxiety. The aroma diffused in the waiting room is calming. The kindness in the tone of our reception staff goes a long way to ensure that women feel more at ease during their consultations.

'Success is liking yourself, liking what you do and liking how you do it,' is a quote of Maya Angelou's that really resonates with me. I have been one of the fortunate cohort of people who love their job. I do believe that it is a chicken-and-egg cycle, and the more you enjoy your work, the more you build motivation and excellence becomes your brand.

I recognise an obvious gap in the way women's health care is delivered in that few private gynaecologists and obstetricians provide their services through a multidisciplinary team care setting. I feel the days of solo practitioners managing women's health care needs are well and truly over. Nowadays, best clinical practice means harnessing skills and opinions of a group of cohesive clinicians empowered by digital technology.

I know we are setting a standard that becomes the norm for women, and we have so much interest from clinicians setting up their practices and highlighting the advantage of collaborative care at every opportunity.

Although there can be multiple clinicians renting rooms or geographically co-located, the advantage of a patient-centric integrated care model is obvious when clinicians communicate via advanced technological connections as well as face-to-face discussions and meetings.

My draft model, created on a handwritten piece of paper, empowered women into the driving seats of their health journeys. It included the use of some digital-based resources to enhance consent and shared decision-making.

We provide evidence-based information to enhance general understanding of the specific pathology that the patient is diagnosed with, plus information around all options of care available with pros and cons highlighted can enable this to occur.

The good thing about caring for women, especially my niche of looking after midlife women, especially in the context of management of heavy menstrual bleeding and menopause, is that I look after a lot of women that I can relate to. This connection is so powerful.

Women's health has been riddled with taboo and shame for so long that it is critical that safe spaces are created for them moving forward. I see that generational change every day in my practice, where many patients will articulate that they got little information from their mothers or that it was not accepted culture to discuss women's health issues. I am so pleased that women are now more open to hold discussions with their children to ensure that they have better experiences.

Young teenagers coming with their mothers and fathers to access health care gives me comfort that as a society we aim to do better – we aim to diagnose endometriosis early and minimise unplanned pregnancies by providing access and education around contraceptive choices.

We aim to provide better stability and recognition of mental health during reproductive times, both for men and women; we aim to minimise cervical cancer by participating in a robust national cervical cancer program. The focus on pelvic floor integrity and benefit of timely pelvic floor exercises and care emphasise the role of allied health physiotherapy. We pride ourselves on having the preventative care lens in addition to treating or managing existing conditions.

So how did this dream of mine materialise? What are the ingredients for a successful practice? How does one balance the reality of overheads when it comes to a boutique, digitally sophisticated medical centre? I am naturally attracted to high-end equipment and want to provide our patients access to the best possible arrangement in this regard.

However, that does come at significant cost, and this means that it is mostly a private model. We became so busy because of the lack of streamlined arrangements offering multiple services under one roof. Many of the women we care for are time-poor and appreciate tandem appointments minimising time off work.

We care for many interstate patients, and our practice's business plan includes developing a service pathway model to support patients from rural and regional Australia. Fortunately, these patients have the opportunity to access procedural gynaecological medical care in the women's health space.

As a woman of colour, opportunities are not handed out to

you on a plate. There are patriarchal systemic structures at various points of one's career that need to be negotiated, and my wish for the young ones who come behind us is to access a more level playing field for all.

One has a choice between victim mode and aiming to fall forward. I chose the latter, and the reality is that the energy you put out into the universe is the same energy you receive back. It is so important to believe in yourself and have clarity of vision. Few are just 'lucky' to achieve success. For most of us, it means years of hard work and focus. Again, if you are passionate about your work, it makes the working day fun, and the icing on the cake is when the team around you is compassionate and cohesive.

Women of colour are invisible to general society. The stories my patients tell me are of those who felt trivialised in the workforce. Their talents are less valued. Managers are often perceived to be more privileged and capable than them. They often start the consultation with an apology!

One thing that I have noted anecdotally is how women of colour undoubtedly off their strength via connections. This is a strategy that worked for me personally. No doubt women are connecting over social media platforms (a favourite of mine is 'Grumpy Medical Mums' on Facebook), and from those friendships over the airwaves or keyboards, many relationships are formed.

The confidence that women experience can now be gained virtually as well as in person, which suits the digital landscape tenfold. Social media can offer safe spaces for them when used sensibly. No doubt this is a way in which many barriers that women of colour face are overcome.

Diversity is the future, and we are moving (thankfully) towards a more balanced one – judging by the number of women who were sworn into parliament at the recent election. And of course, intersectionality matters as gender is simply one of the many angles in the analytical framework for explaining how aspects of a person's identity combine to create different modes of discrimination and privilege.

I would like to end by communicating once more, believe in yourself and dare to dream strategically. Identify a need in society that you are passionate about. For me, it is the high of caring for the women with heavy menstrual bleeding (HMB). They often come to me iron depleted and anaemic, not to mention exhausted. We need to ensure there is no underlying malignancy or pre-malignancy contributing to the abnormal menstrual cycles.

There are many medical and surgical methods to avoid heavy loss. As I say, it is 'a problem with many solutions', and once we have worked through the best-fit option, the patient is reassured. A version of herself that had been buried underneath all the suffering from the HMB is revealed.

This is one example of why I am a proud woman in the medical system; so that I can help move women from dark spaces riddled with pain, bleeding and tiredness to a new improved baseline for them. A lot of the power for positive change is in the hands of our wonderful community of general practitioners.

I often wonder why women wait so long with treatable problems prior to seeking help. We also receive a lot of second opinion consults as well as patient reviews, who have sought help from multiple practitioners in the past. So, this is a complex issue, where women are not always offered timely medical options that would improve their status quo a lot faster.

Our medical centre is nearly unique in that we have invited general practitioners with a special interest in women's health into the clinical team to add to the list of services. I am aware of large GP medical centres having non-GP specialists visiting them to do some sessions onsite, but do not know of obstetrics and gynaecology-based practices doing this in reverse.

The advantage for us having a wider pool of contracted clinicians is that the primary care lens is also included in the way the team operates, and this is a really important angle. It is sad to see the decline in GP morale and numbers of younger doctors who are not keen to embark on this path for a career, worsened no doubt by the toll of the COVID-19 pandemic burnout.

We are hoping to have some training positions to allow registrars to upskill in the breadth of women's health as well as be a way we can give back to society. It also means that these new standards in women's health are accepted as routine instead of such an unusual arrangement as it currently is.

In addition, we often have work experience students (our reception staff have asked fondly if we are running a high school!), and again I want them to see how women can care for women, the representation I so often did not see.

We host elective medical students both domestic and from overseas, and in our practice the patients have been so gracious of their inclusion, which is wonderful to see.

I thought we may have more women declining to have a medical student sit in or learn, especially as this is a mostly private model, but the vast majority of patients consent happily to this.

They can see the vibe of the medical centre is community centric, which is also what our patients are. At the end of the day, when setting up any business or project, we have to start with defining our *why* as per the famous author and international speaker Simon Sinek. Once that is sorted all else will fall into place!

So many women I care for are overwhelmed by all the roles they are performing at work and in their personal lives. Perhaps these women have neglected their own wellbeing in the process. It is a pleasure to care for them with a dedicated team and highlight that the carer role (be it for fur babies, work commitments, children and/or aging parents) is important but her own wellbeing must come first!

I admit it is a generalisation, but women often do not prioritise their own needs, and I am hoping our team achieves its basic mission of raising awareness and breaking these cycles for women. As I say countless times during a working day, 'But you are important too,' or, 'I appreciate all you are doing for others but who is looking after you?'

So, all you champions reading this book, your time is now!

Quality of life is vital for yourself and if you are a clinician, the same goes for the community of patients we serve.

Be the change.

Jump through hoop after hoop.

Adjust your crown.

Embrace diversity.

Surround yourself with like-minded friends, especially other supportive women.

Let go of those that bring you down. After all, life is too short to waste time and energy with people who don't raise you up.

Find your tribe and create a more balanced tomorrow.

We have a picture in our reception of a massive entrance, with our hashtag *#makeyourowndoor*. And indeed, that is the advice to all, from a woman of colour who has smashed many a glass ceiling, if a door does not open for you, simply make another and open it instead!

It is the new normal.

DR M TALAT UPPAL

Dr Talat Uppal is an obstetrician and gynaecologist who currently works both at the Northern Beaches and Hornsby Ku-ring-gai hospitals as a visiting medical officer.

She is the director of Women's Health Road and has set up an innovative integrated multidisciplinary model with a strong patient-centred approach to women's health care.

Her niche interest is the management of women with heavy menstrual bleeding especially around perimenopause.

She is also a clinical senior lecturer in obstetrics and gynaecology at Northern Medical School, University of Sydney.

Her previous decade-long role was based at Manly and Mona Vale Hospitals, as a senior obstetrics staff specialist and clinical director of women's, children and family health.

She is the past chair of both the NSW State Reference Committee and NSW RANZCOG Education Subcommittee.

She is a fellow of the Australian Association for Quality in Health Care as well as a fellow of the Australasian College of Health Service Management.

She is the past coordinator of Diploma (DRANZCOG) OSCE examination as her educational passion is supporting the role of general practitioners in the Women's health context.

She is one of the RANZCOG media spokespersons.

She is fluent in three languages and has much overseas exposure with volunteer teaching work.

womenshealthroad.com.au

CEO BRANDING FOR SUCCESS

Hazel Herrington

Listen up, ladies. It's time to take over the business world – one brand at a time. That's right, we're talking about CEO branding. And no, this doesn't mean wearing a power suit and carrying a briefcase everywhere you go (although that could help). CEO branding is all about using your personal brand to build a successful business.

Now, you may be thinking, *I don't even have a personal brand. How can I possibly create a CEO brand?* But we're here to tell you that it's not as difficult as you might think. In fact, with a little planning and execution, anyone can create a killer CEO brand.

So, what exactly is a CEO brand? A CEO brand is a public persona that you present to the world. It's how you want people to see you and your business. Essentially, it's your business' identity.

It is no secret that a company's CEO is one of the most important aspects of its branding and marketing strategy. To create a successful, recognisable brand, the CEO must be onboard and understand the importance of their role in representing the company. Branding is so much more than just a logo or slogan – it's the heart and soul of your business. It's what sets you apart from your competition and defines how customers perceive you. A strong brand will instil trust and loyalty in your customers, while a weak brand will repel them. Your brand is everything from your company name and logo to your mission statement, values and culture.

However, many business owners and CEOs alike make common mistakes when it comes to their branding which can ultimately lead to a less successful business. Research has shown that business owners who have a clear understanding of branding are two times more likely to experience significant growth in their business.

What is business branding & why is it important?

Business branding is the process of creating a unique identity for your business. This identity includes your business name, logo, tagline and other visual elements. Your brand should be consistent across all platforms, from your website to your social media accounts. There are many benefits to business branding. A strong brand can help you attract new customers, build customer loyalty and stand out from your competition. A well-branded business is also more valuable, so it's important to consider branding when you're planning for the future of your business.

As the CEO, you are the face of your business and play a vital role in its branding. Therefore, it's important to take the time to create a personal brand that aligns with your company's values and mission. This will help you build trust and credibility with customers, as well as attract top talent to your business.

Here are some tips for creating a personal brand as a CEO:

- Define your target audience: Who are you trying to reach with your branding? Knowing your target audience is essential for crafting a message that resonates with them.
- Be authentic: Customers can spot inauthenticity from a mile away. Be genuine in your interactions and honest about what your business stands for.
- Be consistent: Consistency is key when it comes to branding. Make sure all of your marketing materials, from your website to your social media posts, reflect your brand identity.
- Tell your story: Share your company's story with customers and employees to humanise your business and build a connection with them.
- Be passionate: Showcase your passion for your business and industry to inspire others.
- Be responsive: In today's fast-paced world, it's important to be responsive to customer inquiries and feedback. This shows that you care about your customers and are committed to providing them with the best possible experience.
- Be a thought leader: Share your insights and expertise on industry trends to position yourself as a thought leader in your field.
- Be active on social media: Social media is a powerful tool for business branding. Use it to share your story, connect with customers and build relationships with other thought leaders in your industry.
- Invest in professional branding: While you can do some business branding on your own, it's often worth investing in professional help. A branding agency can help you create a strong, cohesive brand that will help you achieve your business goals.

Common branding blunders

There are many common mistakes businesses make when branding that can hurt their growth. Avoid these branding mistakes to ensure your business is set up for success:

Not defining the brand

The first step to successfully branding your business is to sit down and define what your brand is. What are your core values? What message do you want to communicate? What feeling do you want your customers to have when they think of your company? If you cannot answer these basic questions, it will be very difficult to create a coherent brand strategy.

Trying to be all things to all people

Another common mistake made in business branding is trying to be all things to all people. It is important to remember that your brand is not for everyone, and that's okay! Trying to appeal to too broad of an audience will only result in a diluted message that fails to connect with anyone. It is far better to focus on a specific target market and craft a message that resonates with them.

Failing to stay consistent

Once you have defined your brand and found your target market, it is important to stay consistent with your message. This means using the same colours, fonts and overall aesthetic across all of your marketing materials. It also means maintaining a consistent tone and voice in your communications. Customers should be able to easily recognise your brand, no matter where they see it.

Not putting the CEO front and centre

As we mentioned before, your CEO is one of the most important aspects of your business branding. Unfortunately, many companies make the mistake of hiding their CEO behind a logo or making them inaccessible to the public. A great CEO should be approachable and personable, so make sure they are involved in your branding strategy.

Relying too much on advertising
While advertising can be a great way to get the word out about your brand, it should not be your only marketing strategy. Advertising is often expensive and difficult to measure, so it should only be used as one piece of your larger branding strategy. Instead, focus on creating organic content and building relationships with influencers in your industry.

Ignoring the competition
It's important to keep an eye on what other companies in your industry are doing so you can stay ahead of the curve. Pay attention to their branding strategies and see what you can learn from them. You may even find some inspiration for your own company!

Not measuring results
It's important to set specific goals for your branding strategy and then track your progress over time. This will help you determine what is working and what needs to be improved. Without measuring your results, it will be difficult to know if your branding strategy is successful.

Not investing enough time or money in the brand
Branding is an important part of any business, yet many companies fail to invest the time or money necessary to create a strong brand. A well-defined brand can help you attract new customers, stand

out from your competition and increase your overall profitability. Yet many companies treat branding as an afterthought, instead of a key part of their business strategy. If you want your business to succeed, it's important to invest the time and resources necessary to create a strong brand.

Not being unique

In today's competitive business world, it's more important than ever to be unique. If you want your business to succeed, it's important to find a way to differentiate yourself from your competition. This could mean offering unique products or services, having a different brand identity or anything else that sets you apart from the rest.

Failing to keep up with technology

In today's fast-paced world, it's important to stay up to date with the latest trends and technologies. This includes everything from social media to website design to SEO. If you fall behind, your competition will quickly overtake you.

Not getting help from professionals

Many companies make the mistake of trying to handle their branding in-house. While there's nothing wrong with this, it's often best to leave branding to the professionals. Hiring a branding agency can help ensure that your branding strategy is on point and that you're making the most of your marketing budget.

Failing to create a unique selling proposition

Your unique selling proposition is what sets your business apart from the competition. It's what makes you special and memorable in the minds of your customers. Yet many companies fail to create a strong USP, resulting in a bland and uninspiring brand. If you want your business to succeed, it's important to create a USP that is both unique and compelling.

Not defining the brand's personality

Every brand has a personality, whether it's friendly, serious or somewhere in-between. Without a clear personality, your brand will be forgettable and uninteresting.

Relying on gut feeling rather than data

In business, it's important to make decisions based on data, not gut feeling. Relying on your gut when it comes to branding can lead to making poor decisions that could negatively impact your business. Be sure to base your decisions on hard data, not just a hunch.

Failing to constantly evolve

The business world is constantly changing, which means your branding strategy needs to change as well. Many companies make the mistake of failing to evolve their brand over time. This can lead to a stale and outdated brand that fails to connect with customers. To avoid this, it's important to review your branding strategy regularly and make changes as needed.

Not incorporating feedback

Feedback from customers is essential for any business, yet many companies fail to incorporate it into their branding strategy. It's important to listen to what customers are saying and use it to improve your brand.

Not protecting the brand

Your business brand is one of your most valuable assets. Not protecting your brand can include everything from failing to trademark your logo to not monitoring how your brand is being used online. Take steps to protect your business brand, and you'll be able to avoid costly mistakes that could damage your business.

Not knowing when to rebrand

There are times when it's necessary to rebrand your business. This can be due to a change in business strategy or a change in the market. Failing to rebrand can result in being stuck with a brand that no longer represents your business. If you're unsure whether you should rebrand, it's best to consult with a branding expert.

Not networking

Many business owners fail to realise the importance of networking. Networking is essential for any business, especially when it comes to branding. When you network with other business owners, you'll be able to share ideas and learn about new branding strategies. This can help you keep your branding strategy fresh and up to date.

Here are five examples of CEOs that have successfully branded themselves and their businesses:

1. Mark Zuckerberg, CEO of Facebook.
2. Bill Gates, CEO of Microsoft.
3. Jeff Bezos, CEO of Amazon.
4. Larry Page, CEO of Google.
5. Sergey Brin, Co-Founder of Google.

By following their footsteps, you too can develop a strong and successful business brand and achieve corporate success.

HAZEL HERRINGTON

Hazel is a global leader and woman empowerment champion. As an entrepreneur, motivational speaker and author, she has been recognised as one of the most influential women in the world by several prestigious organisations.

Hazel has been a driving force in the global women's empowerment movement, striving to break down the barriers that limit women's potential. She is a strong advocate for equal opportunity and gender equality and has worked tirelessly to promote these values around the world. Hazel's work in the field of women's empowerment has helped countless women realise their own strength and equip them to become economically independent and wholly sufficient through her two charities Destiny Arise and I Am Bible Distribution.

Hazel is also a successful entrepreneur, having founded and led several businesses to success. She is the founder and CEO of Herrington Publications Worldwide publishing and marketing company that produces the popular *Inspiring Women* magazines *I Am Woman Global*, *Lady Politico Power*, and *Lady Global Power* which are distributed in over 130 countries to over twenty-five million viewers. Hazel has been an invaluable resource to women all over the world, providing them with the tools and resources they need to achieve their dreams. Her expertise is in the areas of business and leadership development, women's empowerment and entrepreneurship.

Hazel is a powerful motivational speaker, sharing her story of overcoming adversity to inspire others to reach their full potential. She has spoken at numerous conferences and events around the world which include the following:

- Forbes School of Business & Technology, International Women's Day with the former President of Mauritius HE Madame President Dr Ameenah Gurib-Fakim.
- The Pearls of Africa Women Leadership Conference held by Berkeley Middle East Holdings and hosted by the Royal Family Investment Advisor Musa Shaik.
- 'Achieving SDGs through entrepreneurship and innovation' Women Entrepreneurship Congress 2020 held by Female Innovators Hub with the former President of Mauritius HE Madame President Dr Ameenah Gurib-Fakim.
- NAC 2018 Australia with Tony Robbins.
- B Squared 2017 Australia with Gary Vee.

Hazel has also interviewed and met the following Hollywood celebrities:

BUSINESS DOMINATION

- Hollywood actor and director Mel Gibson at Mega Success.
- Hollywood actor Charlie Sheen at Mega Success.
- Hollywood actor and comedian Jason Alexander from the iconic sitcom *Seinfeld*.
- Grammy Award nominee Jewel Kilcher at Mega Success.
- Hollywood A-list actor Mark Wahlberg.
- Hollywood actress Brooke Shields.
- Hollywood A-list actor Michael Douglas.
- TV reality star Bethany Frankel.
- Musician Brett Michaels.
- Apple co-founder Steve Wozniak.
- Former advisor to President Donald Trump George Ross.
- Musician Gene Simmons.

Hazel has received the following global awards and nominations:

- G100 Mission million – Australia Country Chair Brand Creation & Marketing.
- 2021 Top 100 Most Successful Women Award - Bahrain Women Entrepreneurs club.
- 2021 Top 1% Global Exemplary Leaders Award winner – certifyme.online.
- Global Entrepreneurship and Community Award winner – Zim Achievers.
- Pan African Thrive Legend Award – Voices of Water award winner – JB Dondolo Inc.
- Gold Coast Australia Woman of the Year nominee with Harvey Norman.
- Australia Top 100 Women of Influence with Qantas and *Australian Financial Review* nominee.

- AusMumpreneur Multicultural Award nominee.

SHOWING UP AS YOUR AUTHENTIC SELF

Jane Vandermeer

I knew that it was time to stop. I was exhausted. I felt like a salmon swimming upstream. The eternal optimist that I am knew that it was time to take myself out of the equation. The empath in me forever wanted to help. Finally, I realised that I needed to put myself first. So, I resigned from a well-paying job towards a future unknown. I knew that I needed some time off. The continual migraines were relentless. The neck pain was constant. If I am honest, I haven't been able to move my neck properly since against the immeasurable pain that continues. I had been working ten hours a day, seven days a week, for eighteen months.

Next, I experienced not one, but two serious cancer scares.

The burnout of adrenal fatigue was looming. Yet the straw that broke the camel's back, so to speak, wasn't the health scares or the peer bullying that comes with the fashion industry, but the client that pushed me to my edge. No matter how hard we tried, nothing made him happy.

There was no time or space to reflect. The pressure never let up. I asked myself constantly, *What is balance?*

So, I took myself out of the situation. I remember thinking a week or two of rest should do the trick. How wrong I was. My phone stayed on silent for four months. I screened every single call. I had constant debilitating migraines and I got sicker. However, this epiphany was life-changing.

I couldn't be more grateful for that time in my life.

Life is so fast. The pace is addictive. Once you are on the hamster wheel, how do you get off? If you take yourself off the wheel, what happens next? Does someone younger, more motivated, more current and fresher take your place?

Somewhere along the way, to keep up or keep one step ahead, we lose ourselves. I remember seeing my kinesiologist practitioner. She said, 'Are you aware that you keep holding your breath? When you breathe, it's like you are in a flight-or-fight mode.'

This had become such innate behaviour. I had no idea that I was doing that.

I always knew that I was a great multitasker. As many women are. Combine that with the people-pleaser part of my personality, and it becomes a deadly concoction. If a client contacted me out of hours or was desperate for help, I would always do my best to help them, even though it was harming me. It is because of this work ethic I was successful in business; however, my body was telling me something else.

My default setting became pushing myself to fit 'one more thing in' each day. Before I knew it, the thrill of another sale or happy client was the space I sat in. Did I mention that I was on 100% commission at that point? More on that later.

Filling every single moment quickly became 'normal' for me.

What I didn't realise was, bit by bit, I was losing connection to myself. My intuition. My stillness. My creativity. Bit by bit I was sitting in 'doing and action' and not creating or allowing space to 'just be'.

A result of remaining within this state of 'doing' or continually stretched beyond okay, is we defer our emotions. We ignore our red flags. We know it's harmful, but we push ahead anyway. We keep going. We keep pushing.

I had a severely bulged disc in my lower back. I could barely walk. Even as I write this, it seems so obvious, but at the time, when I was in the situation, I was clouded in pain. Feeling the 'should' but not the 'stop' button was an unhelpful pattern I created. I knew I was letting people down, but I was also letting myself down by not listening. However, I went to work. I had four client appointments that day. The 'good and polite girl' in me didn't want to cancel appointments at the eleventh hour.

So, in-between each appointment, I lay down under my desk.

This experience was a wonderful opportunity to take myself out of the equation. My body was screaming, *This is enough, and you need a break. You need to 'be' for a while. You need to heal.*

So, I rested in bed for a day or two and went right back to work to attend to my other commitments the day after.

This opportunity gave me so many examples of a life that I had no idea about. I learnt that I didn't need to sit in (or default back to) flight-or-fight mode constantly. I can now see, looking back, that I was functioning within flight-or-fight mode for much of my adult life and career. It is no wonder that at a certain point my body crumbled.

This unravelling gave me the time and space to 'unlearn' old behaviours. I did default back to workaholic behaviour. That is what we are taught to do, isn't it? Work hard until we drop.

During those times, all the things that keep me balanced, that keep me 'Jane', went by the wayside. I was ignoring exercise, creativity and good food. Instead, I consumed more coffee, more sugar and treats.

The effect and the addiction of flight-or-flight mode felt impossible to escape.

A few years later, I had another opportunity to listen to the 'whispers of my intuition'. Two separate cancer scares, adrenal fatigue, bullying, unable to move my neck properly and continual severe migraines finally floored me.

Okay, body, I am listening.

However, at this point, I still thought a week or so would do the trick. How naive of me!

Although this sounds extreme, I won't lie, because it was the biggest wake-up call of my life.

To be honest, I didn't have many answers at that point about moving forward. I did know that I wanted to be back in small business again. I knew that I needed a break from being a boss. I questioned if there could be a different way to function, but I had no idea how.

It was a very uncomfortable feeling not knowing all the answers. I have always felt clarity in my life and now I wasn't sure of anything. I knew that I still loved fashion and couldn't ever imagine walking away from it, however, I needed a break.

As I was so used to being insanely busy, I started doing online courses during this time. I couldn't just be still. It took a very long time to settle within myself, but eventually I got there.

I think that we are given the guidance we need at the time we need. We are given little drops of clarity. Usually not the whole picture, but moments of unique insight. At the time, I wanted answers and reassurance to focus my energy.

It was incredibly uncomfortable not having all of the answers. However, it's in these moments that answers can surface.

What I didn't realise was that this was one of the most important lessons for me to learn. Bit by bit. I would think to myself, *Jane, slow down and create space. Don't fill the diary.*

Anxiety has the nasty way of sneaking up on us. However, this concept is like a muscle. The more we practice, the easier it becomes. But it was often very uncomfortable. Many days I felt like it was one step forward, five steps back!

Now my adrenals are happy and no more cancer cells in sight. The stress in my life is viewed very differently, and that applies to my business life too.

Eventually, I stopped being so hard on myself. I had my whole adult career of patterns that had evolved, so undoing those patterns was going to take time.

Young dreams and motivation

Fashion has always been in my blood. It was never a decision, but a natural progression. I started my first business at sixteen years old, making pretty gowns for my peers.

I always knew that I wanted to do big things within the fashion industry. However, I had no idea how I would do that. My very romantic imagination fulfilled that part of me. Mixing with glamorous women and going to fashion shows was all the inspiration I needed. Working with very high-end fabrics and travelling the world became a way of life.

Beautiful buildings, foreign lands and languages, well beyond my current world, was the life I had been seeking. I had always dreamt of becoming a fashion designer or a buyer travelling the world. Life felt limitless. I also knew that I wanted to lead my own business. At the time, I had no idea how, but I just knew it was for me. Even though I was quite shy and unassertive, I always had big dreams.

I started sewing at nine years old and it was my beautiful creative mum who taught me. I did attend an academic school at the time, but it wasn't massively creative. I remember in year ten, my textile teacher asked me to teach the class for her. So, from time to time I would teach sewing and textiles 101. However, it wasn't challenging me.

I would go into expensive clothing shops, turn garments inside out to try and work out how things were made. Then I would replicate this at home. That's how I learnt how to do a French seam (this is where the raw edge is enclosed). So, I essentially reverse-engineered the construction.

Even as I write this, I can see that understanding the challenge of construction is a reflection of how my mind works. I look at things from a completely different perspective, attempting to understand why things are the way they are. For example, if you put a bust dart into a garment, you can automatically see how it affects the fit.

I can now see that I've always had an inquisitive mind.

Years later, I graduated with a Bachelor in Fashion at RMIT. My dream had come true. I went to university to learn how to 'do things properly and professionally'. This renowned university, RMIT, created a well-rounded knowledge base.

Naivety & self-belief

I started my couture design business straight from college whilst working for another designer I really admired. I remember thinking, *I can't believe that I can be paid to do what I love. I would do this for free if I had to!*

Within six months, I realised that I needed to bring staff

onboard to help me so that business could continue growing. This made me grow up – and fast! My staff were always many years older than me, as were my clients. However, I could present and speak in a professional way, and people responded to this side of me.

Before long, I realised that women needed help with styling themselves. I realised that what I thought was completely obvious actually wasn't. Many lovely professional women I worked with needed help and guidance, in a kind and non-judgemental way. These skills aren't innate for everyone. My clients were absolutely extraordinary women. They were and are leaders in their respective fields, however, many lacked confidence with their personal presentation.

So, I created many intimate workshops teaching about body shape, colour palettes and styling. I absolutely loved this. It was a blend of all of my skills, and I knew that I was making a massive impact in women's lives. I could see that as my approach was nurturing and non-judgemental, I really made deep changes in women's lives.

Most of my clients came back season after season, year after year. Of course, somewhere along the way, the blend of business and friendship soon follows. Creating the space to truly listen to people was an incredible purpose for me. Seeing beyond what they were actually saying was the gold in my day. To build sincere relationships is a joy. Many people don't actually listen, but these women did. They were waiting for a break in the conversation so that they could talk more about themselves, which so many women never have a true chance to do.

Throughout this time in my couture business, I styled celebrities, and I always thought that was my calling.

After dressing A-list celebs and seeing my creations on the

front page of the media, I realised that this market wasn't my true love. I am a much more private person than the tabloids required. I prefer to work with women who, like me, are a little less in the public eye.

A lady I dressed for ten years is now a good friend, and this represents the magic of fashion and friendship. Rose was extremely accomplished within her career. She was university educated and had started studying for her PhD. Travelling the world and earning great money was a normal day for her. However, she wasn't an off-the-rack size. Rose had a bust AU size 16, waist size 12 and hips size 24. She was very self-conscious about her hips and bottom. All of her clothes were loose and baggy as a way of shielding her from herself. Soon, however, Rose trusted my ideas.

I showed her better colours, the right shapes, fabrics and textures to show off her tiny waist, but within an aesthetic that was true to her personality. As time progressed, her whole demeanour changed. This shy person really started to blossom. It was a great honour to play such a part in her personal journey. My approach has always been to not just 'tell women what to wear' but to teach and help them understand why. It is when you understand the *why* that real change can occur. I appreciate that we all learn differently.

However, most of us need to see a visual. We need to see the right shape or colour, and then the wrong version. It is at that point, when we are armed with logical information, that true authenticity and empowerment can happen.

Becoming a small business owner so young was a blend of naivety and self-belief. If I didn't understand a new concept, then I simply taught myself. If I couldn't find a garment for a client, we would make it in-house.

I have grown up with both of my parents in their respective

small businesses. I understood that, ultimately, I am responsible for my clients' happiness, staff motivation and growth of the business. So, I took it upon myself to become a good generalist. I needed to basically understand all aspects of small business. I also realised that I have an inquisitive mind, so I like to understand why things are the way that they are. I needed to understand the main concepts. There were, of course, some epic fails. So often I would fall in a heap, let the tears flow, beat myself up and probably eat chocolate. Then try again tomorrow.

When I was younger, I basically thought we were more or less the same – fashion and me. However, as time has progressed, I have realised that I don't think in a linear fashion. I have the ability to think and view things from many different perspectives at once.

Partly this is being a creative thinker as well an entrepreneurial one.

We need the balance of linear thinking for business spreadsheets and costs. I have realised that the ability to think from different perspectives also allows me the ability to problem-solve. I also believe that this is a skill required for small business. We need to think ahead, not just wait for things to happen. Problem-solving on the fly is a vital part of a small business mindset, and I have it in droves.

Consider all options, make a decision and move forward. Don't waste lots of energy reliving decisions or second-guessing ourselves. I have done my fair share of second-guessing, however, it is ultimately a waste of energy and clogs up my mind.

I thought that I would have my couture business for the rest of my life, however, at a certain point, I knew that I needed to keep growing. To be honest, I had no idea of my next steps but I knew that it was time. I needed to keep growing and challenging myself. So, I sold that business and took some time out.

Dreams & adventures

As a motivated person, I did want some level of certainty or clarity on my next steps, yet I didn't have it. I did know that I needed some time to myself; I needed time away from customer service.

As well as my love of fashion design, a super big dream of mine was to become a fashion buyer. However, I didn't really ever think that it might be possible. Buyers seemed so glamorous and well-travelled, and I doubted if this was the role for me.

However, opportunities present themselves in life. Often, they are super scary. But somewhere in there, I did have belief in myself and my abilities (mixed in with lots of self-doubt).

We are complex, aren't we?

I started working part-time in a retail fabric shop for a while. I passionately love high-end fabrics, so this was a dream. Within a couple of months, their sales agent resigned. So, I made time and created a little presentation as to why I would be perfect for the role. I didn't exactly have the experience. But in my mind, why on earth would I go for a role that I could already do? I wanted a role where I could challenge myself to learn and then hopefully thrive in. I knew that I had enough skills and knowledge but most of all passion and drive to do the role.

With a blend of (again) naivety and self-belief, I went on 100% commission with no retainer. I never once regretted that decision. It wasn't long before I was the top Australian and Asian agent and head buyer.

The very first time I arrived at the famous International Fabric Trade Fair in Paris, Premiere Vision it was a monumental moment! I stood there and didn't know whether to laugh or burst into tears. I thought to myself, *I have finally made it.*

Really, all I have ever done is give things a go. Work to my strengths and be brave. When I don't know something, I learn.

I am always open to learning and aim to avoid rigid thinking. I always believe that we must find people we can learn from. This is such valuable advice that I cultivated along the way.

For approximately ten years, opportunities felt effortless. If I had known all of this when I was younger, it would probably have felt too overwhelming and intimidating. I love when we are following our path, we receive 'breadcrumbs' of opportunities along the way. I thrive on the forks in the road that are there to challenge us. There would have been nothing wrong with me keeping my couture business my whole adult life.

But look what I would have missed out on if I didn't dare to dream.

Flight-or-fight became my thing!

Next came the wall that changed my life: adrenal fatigue, two serious cancer scares, constant migraines, stiff neck and a bulged disc where I was unable to walk.

Sounds fantastic, doesn't it?

I thought that I would just need a few weeks to get back on top of things. My phone went silent for around four months. It was time to create 'super-duper' boundaries whilst I was so unwell.

Well that actually took a couple of years.

During this time, I created another business: Intuitive Whispers.

The name is reflective of 'listening to the whispers of our intuition'. Again, this business name was a culmination of my passions and skills. Soon after, I created a natural deodorant line that I called Breast Care Deodorant.

This was never going to be a business as such, but created just for me, family and friends. I began to design pretty labels and packaging which I loved. My love of beautiful and premium products, mixed with my new knowledge and understanding of health, was making me so happy. I also knew that it would benefit other women.

My innate business head and skills soon kicked in. Within a few months, I was wholesaling this special product.

When I was a buyer, I would usually add a few days onto each trip to explore the local city. On a trip to Paris, I decided to enrol in a perfume making and blending course. Again, this was just for creativity. Well, a few years later, these skills came in handy. Next, I created perfume oils that became part of the range. These off-the-cuff special products won me eighteen national awards within the natural beauty space. Next was my first international award, 'Luxury Artisan Perfume Brand of the Year 2021', by a UK company. It was this award that drew the attention of *Vogue UK*, who then approached me to feature the products.

This whole thing was a very interesting experience. It wasn't really ever a conscious decision to create that business. But what I was starting to do during that time was approach life in a very different way.

I also realised after I got very sick, that I could create a life and business differently and tip traditional business formulas on their heads. I had come from a world that did not appreciate – let alone value – empathy and sensitivity. It was seen as a weakness, and that the only way was to push and 'hustle' constantly, meet targets and not blow budgets.

I slowly realised that there was a different way. A more balanced way.

Sometimes, business needs us to be proactive. We are driven by a masculine energy, however, that needs to be balanced. Yet, surrendering to a different pace can be seen as not ambitious enough, especially within the fashion industry.

My approach to personal styling is very holistic and abundant.

Rather than making my clients solely reliant on me, I empower them to find the answers. I give them the tools to fly.

My solution is working with women over a longer period of time, which is why I created a bespoke five-month program. This is how real change, personal growth and professional skills are learned – by refining the finesse.

Fashion, style & self-worth

Another 'drip-feed' benefit that I didn't realise at the time was that I was given the opportunity to connect to my body again. To get out of my head. To work out what I feel, not just what I think.

I have always been highly intuitive and sensitive. However, many, many people over my adult life would make comments such as, 'You are so sensitive, toughen up,' always with the inference that it was a negative trait.

Well, bit by bit, during my healing phase, I realised my sensitivity and intuition is actually my superpower. However, getting to this point was such a process. Again, unlearning all that I had been told.

But how on earth does all of this fit into my world and love of fashion?

This bit was much harder. I have always kept the two aspects of myself quite separate. Fashion and styling are about the external – our aesthetic. Intuition and sensitivity are about our inner world. I realised this while on a trip to Europe when I had time and space to reflect. I had always kept my two loves very compartmentalised. Oddly, the two industries don't really have anything to do with one another.

However, I finally realised that these are all my gifts. My innate and refined gifts. So, I planned to combine my business and authentic self.

You know the old saying, 'tick a box'? Well, I was determined to create a new box.

My energy, patience, message, non-judgemental support and emotional tone now shine through. Women are often drawn to me and sometimes they are not sure why.

I think that it is my inner work, peace and skills that acts like a 'safe magnet'.

My perspectives of holistic fashion and personal styling are so much more than guiding you to your perfect colour palette. I want to build my clients' self-worth and confidence to shine brightly from within. I share knowledge to empower women in a holistic way, sprinkling kindness, support and self-love.

I don't want to frame women to fit a cookie-cutter version of themselves that society will accept. My concept is about harmony.

That is when we walk tall.

We command the room differently. We know that we have got it. We are not fiddling with our outfit. Our outside truly reflects our inside. I empower my clients to learn who they are! When you really embrace who you truly are, through effortless grace and style, your life can open up.

It can become so exhausting trying to keep up the facade. Learning to love our uniqueness, loving ourselves right now and reflecting our inner confidence is the 'look' we need to embrace.

Throughout different stages of life, we can lose our way. We can lose our confidence. We forget to listen to ourselves. We can listen to shop assistants or other people and forget how to listen to our inner voice. We look outside for answers rather than within.

You're a beautiful combination.

Fashion & finesse

The next step in my story is creating a finesse and style consulting business. A holistic personal styling service that helps female founders, speakers, coaches and consultants feel like they can take on the world, share their message and light up from the inside. I do this through a combination of online learning and one-on-one online connection and support for women. My ultimate goal is to give women the tools, confidence and clarity to get dressed every day with ease.

I realised that my services are particularly innovative and seek to redefine the traditional personal styling and professional development markets. I deliver unique experiences by using holistic tools to help women find the right clothes and to love the size they are right now.

I have found that one of the most important skills in my work is the ability to truly listen to my clients from a non-judgemental perspective. I do this by gently guiding clients to a revised, updated and truly authentic aesthetic, one that makes them feel strong, confident and self-assured. I understand that women are multi dimensional whose identities are a tangle of connections to activities, places, interests, values and aspirations.

In my long career, I am most proud of my bravery to build my own holistic personal styling business in the way I want. I had always kept my fashion and spiritual and worlds very separate, since the two industries weren't really aligned. Since then, I have realised that these two worlds are my superpower. By combining the two, I have bravely created my own version of 'Jane's Personal Styling'.

JANE VANDERMEER

Jane Vandermeer is a highly intuitive, gentle and innovative thought leader. She has always had a love for high-end fashion – you could say that it is in her blood.

As a creative and entrepreneurial thinker, she has a thirty-year career within the fashion industry, including designer, tailor, pattern maker, quality control, buyer, wholesale and retail sales, lecturer, business owner and creator.

Throughout her entrepreneurial career, Jane has created and built a number of award-winning businesses within the fashion and creative industries. Starting with a couture design business, styling and creating wardrobes for beautiful women, Jane is a highly accomplished buyer and Australasian sales manager. As a passionate educator, Jane teaches, lectures and inspires tertiary fashion students.

Jane has the ability to truly listen to her clients, from a non-judgemental perspective; gently guiding them to a revised, updated and truly authentic aesthetic.

As someone who has coupled passion and purpose, Jane understands that women are multidimensional. Jane has an innate ability to connect with her clients when they can't always articulate their own needs.

Jane is in tune with trends but a confident individualist when it comes to style.

As a proud brand builder, Jane has also built a number of other businesses; her proudest, 'Intuitive Whisper'. Jane is a multi-award-winning Australian fashion business leader, after launching artisan perfume oils and natural deodorants. As an ethical luxury conscious consumer, Jane heralds her international multi-award-winning business, featured in leading publications including *Vogue UK*.

CREATING A JOB YOU LOVE FROM THE GROUND UP

Karen McDermott

When you align your passion with your purpose and pursue it, filtered through your core values, that is where true business success resides.

For me, business domination means getting the foundations right so they can fully support the journey. My studies were in humanities and I never could have foreseen how that would lead me into publishing. It's easier to put the dots together when you're looking backwards, and I've been doing that recently – reflecting on how I got here – because I've had a lot of success in publishing and I wanted to understand how it happened.

What I thought would take me twenty-five years took me seven. I believe it was because I wasn't so focused on goals. I set intentions for myself and went on the journey to each one, allowing them to grow into bigger things than I had originally intended. I hadn't understood, at the start, how good it could be or how big it could be, as it wasn't in my realm of possibility when I set the intention. For me, it is the journey that I focus on, and because I prioritise joy very highly, it means things happen faster.

I also pour loving intention into the journey. Being a mum of six, I'm constantly surrounded by love and insanity. Lucky for me, love is my power source, so that is the energy I choose to put into everything. With parenthood comes bucketloads of loving energy and I have to be super efficient. It's really important to me, and to my values, that I am there for my kids – able to be with them in school holidays, drop them off and pick them up from school, available for them when they're sick. We moved from Ireland to Australia, with no family here, so I am their family, I'm the constant and I would never compromise that.

So, one day, I had this crazy idea. I was very blessed that I was a mum at home, because if I hadn't been, I would never have had the opportunity to find my purpose, hear my calling and pursue it. If I'd been working nine to five, I would have been dropping the kids off at day care, picking them up at five, making dinner late at night, cleaning the house, maybe hardly at home at all, with no space for anything else, certainly not my purpose. Whereas, I was living the most blessed life, I had the space to hear my calling and I will never take it for granted.

So, I dabbled in the law of attraction and went on to become a master practitioner on the subject and never told anyone. I just thought I would apply it to what I was doing and see where it got me, and if I was successful, I'd then share the secret with others because I don't believe in keeping things to myself. I'm guessing you're the same – as we learn it, we share it. We raise each other up and we go on the journey. We don't always get it right, but when we do, we get it *right*. It's about embracing the journey and having fun with it.

So, I created a job for myself. I came into the publishing industry, as a woman setting up my own publishing business. But I was driven by a purpose. I am story fuelled. I know how stories can connect, heal, educate and inspire. Stories are powerful. That's what gets me out there every day, hearing and sharing stories. That's how I started. My calling was to ensure that people's amazing stories are told.

I started telling stories for my children. When we first came to Australia they didn't know about redback spiders or snakes, as they hadn't grow up with that. At the time, I had a twelve-year-old, a two-and-a-half-year-old and I was just about to have my third. I was thirty-five weeks pregnant with her when we moved here. So I started with a little poetry that became a children's book, and if you go to your local bookstore, it's more than likely there. It's called *Australian Animal Walkabout,* and the kids and I created it around our kitchen table. They would draw. We called them Mamma Macs Homemade Children's Books and we completed about one hundred books. Many of them went on to be properly illustrated and have gone out into the world. But that was the joke. It started with children's books, would you believe?

And then I got 'a calling'; an epiphany, perhaps. It was Whoopi Goldberg's fault. I was watching *The View* and I got the calling to take action over something I was very passionate about. I knew I had to tell my story. So I joined NaNoWriMo (National Novel Writing Month) – totally irrationally, I must add, as I'd just had my fourth child at that time.

She was four weeks old. As she breastfed on one side, I was typing for a whole month with my other hand. She only got one boob that month and I had a fifty-thousand-word novel at the end of it. Where it came from, I have no idea, but it was a catalyst into authorship because I knew nothing about the publishing process. So that's where my passion came from, to help others to tell their stories.

I love what I do, but I work wisely, efficiently using twenty-four hours of the day. I sleep when I need to sleep. I eat when I need to eat. And I'm with my kids when I need to be with them. I'm able to prioritise, and for me, that's my definition of success. I'm very ambitious. I like to achieve things, push the boundaries and find different, out-of-the-box ways to do things. I rarely line up with every one else, I usually find a VIP backstage pass in that way. It's all about connection, and I have met the most amazing people over the past twelve years. It's quite phenomenal. It's amazing what becomes normal in your life as you just set an intention and then wait for what appears in front of you. But you do have to have an open mind to see it. So many people are closed off to the wider view. They think they have to set a goal and work on each stepping stone to reach that goal. But then you're only focused on each stepping stone and you won't see any wider than that.

Personally, I don't even see the stepping stones as I'm too busy up in the clouds, floating and passing everything from a more divine perspective. It's so much more fun that way and I get bigger results. I have parties on my cloud and everyone is welcome to come along for the ride. That's the way I love it. It's not everybody's cup of tea, it can be unpredictable at times, but it's fun. And where there's joy, there's success.

I created the perfect job for me. I used to be a jack-of-all-trades at the beginning. I did everything in my business – apart from editing. I'm not an editor. Editors are amazing. In my eyes, they're the Gods of the publishing industry. But everything else was up to me. I typeset books, created the covers – everything. And then, as I grew up into my business, I suppose I became a big girl. I had to put my big-girl pants on. I started to delegate the stuff that was not in my genius zone so I could do the things I do best. When you get to that point in business, it's a beautiful thing, but you don't start there. I loved doing everything at the beginning, but you kind of know when it's time to start delegating because you start thinking, *Oh, that's painful for me to think about doing right now.* That's when you get someone else to do it. If your love's not in it and your heart's not in it, you're just not giving it your best. Delegate to someone who loves doing it, so they can give it their best, and the job gets done with love. It just makes sense. As you grow, your business grows, your cashflow grows and then you're able to do that. You're able to be a bit more fearless, so embrace that and have the courage to move out of your comfort zone.

The magic happens just outside of that comfort zone. Push yourself just a little bit and you'll discover you're moving forward all the time. You don't have to take a leap, it's often just a little step.

Sometimes your actions may seem irrational to the outside world, but choosing what fills you up every day will keep you energised to achieve more and more without it detracting from what you already have. Create the perfect job for you. It's about you and what lights you up. Find a job in that space and it won't feel like a chore. I've seen too many mums doing jobs they hate because they think that they have to. And I understand that everybody has different circumstances, but that could have been my choice had I not been daring enough to say, *I want to make this work for me.* It could be the stubborn Irishness in me as well. I am going to make this work so I can have the perfect life blend, for me. I'm passionate about what I do, and the stories I help to share can make a difference in our world. I want my kids to learn that our actions mean more than our words. I want to show them what's possible, so they learn to follow their purpose. It's phenomenal to watch the process, when I see them have the courage to take the next step that works for them, regardless of how irrational it may seem to the outside world.

Seeking a job that lights you up is paramount to success. The perfect job is found where there is joy because you can make a business out of anything if you enjoy what you're doing. If you're heart's not in it and you don't enjoy the way you're showing up in the world, your job really ends up being a chore. There are many people who get to the end of their lives and think, *Wow. I didn't do anything with my life.*

From my own experience, I've worked in several jobs where I clocked in and out and had set hours. I did find fulfilment in that, but it wasn't until I discovered a passion for stories, and aligned that with my values of wanting to be a hands-on parent, that I actually found and structured a business around what worked in my life. I created the perfect job for me from a seedling of an idea.

How did I do that?
Well, I set an intention to build a million-dollar press. I took action and started to build the foundations. My studies were in humanities, not in publishing, but I had a passion for stories and it brought me lots of joy to see stories come together in published books. Because I was so passionate about it, I learned so much in a very short period of time. I researched and did a lot of training; everything I needed to do step by step, as I educated myself along the journey.

A big part of creating my job from the ground up was to have clarity and a very clear vision around what it was I wanted to create; what it would look like and who I would serve. Because I was an author before I was a publisher, I could understand my clients' needs from an author's perspective. In any business, I recommend you really get to understand from your clients' perspective what it is they need, so you can give them the best experience and service. I've been on the author's journey and sometimes it's not the most wonderful experience, but when you walk alongside someone through the tough times, as well as the wonderful times, they can value the experience and really value you, because you're not just there for the good times, you're there for the whole journey. In my job, going on the journey means warts and all – it means that we're all in – so there'll be a very deep connection there.

Showing up with the right intentions, laying the foundations for your business in the first few years and focusing on what you know you need to deliver means you can get often get results quickly. You have to have the purpose and passion to lay the foundations, but as soon as things start moving and you need things like procedures and forms that need lawyers to go over them, start bringing that in incrementally so it doesn't become too overwhelming. Do try and stay in your genius zone as much as you can. You definitely need an accountant, so get into the rhythm of having an accountant do your accounts annually and make sure you're ticking all boxes.

Now, at the beginning, you're not going to be in your genius zone all the time, so just work where your strengths are as much as you as possibly can. When you do have to do 'work', do it from a perspective of it being for the greater good and that will keep you motivated. One of my top tips when it comes to doing stuff that doesn't light you up so much is to remember that when you're building something that's worthwhile, you need to learn the ropes and do the things you don't want to do. And you can know that when the time comes, you're going to be able to delegate those jobs and stay in your genius zone. If you look at the flexibility your job and what you're building is bringing into your life, then you will be energised by that. Remember too, on the days when things feel a bit overwhelming, or you're tired, that is not a day to push through, it's a day to pause and close over your to-do list, even if it's only for a few hours.

Even if it's not for the entire day, when you feel overwhelmed, go and do something outside of work that brings you joy, otherwise you'll end up burning out. I regularly go to the beach, meet a friend for coffee or even have a Netflix day. I do something where my brain doesn't have to be in that energy, then when it's time for me to go back and focus on the jobs at hand, I do it with renewed energy, efficiency and excitement for clearing my list because I'm ready to move to the next stage.

It's important to realise, whenever you're building a business, there's going to be struggles alongside the breakthroughs.

It's the same with any journey in life, whether it's business or personal. When you're achieving a lot of things, you're going to have struggles and breakthroughs, so choose your perspective when it comes to challenges. Understand that you are levelling up, so the challenge is not wasted time. It's not a setback, it's actually moving up to the next level of success. That will empower you and energise you to get through the challenge. Sometimes in the struggle, it's a time for action and other times it's not. It's up to you to equip yourself with the 'knowing of what is' at any given time. I often speak of the 'power of knowing'. It's when you go within yourself and all the answers are there and then you lean outside for support to make things happen.

It's not the other way around.

Far too many people are leaning outside looking to others for the answers, which means too many other people are having influence over their success. Whereas, when you learn to connect with your power of knowing, leaning inward for the answers and then outwards for the support, that's where the magic is.

Sharing my story, you can see how I roll – I set the intentions, the inspired thoughts and opportunities present themselves, and then I have to have the courage to say a 'hell yes' to the hell yeses and a 'hell no' when I know it's a NO. Because when you say yes to something that your heart does not agree with, you are doing a disservice not only to yourself, but also to the person you have said yes to.

We're all human and we've all said yes to something that we know is not right. We think we're doing the right thing, when actually, we're not. I was always a yes person. I would have a to-do list of things I didn't want to do. These days, to achieve all the great things I want to achieve in my life, I have to do things unconventionally and with out-of-the-box thinking. I set big fat goals so I have to take actions to make them happen. So whenever I say yes to something and my heart's not in or it's not aligned with where I'm going, then I'm pulling myself away from my goals and intentions. It's also going to create some resentment, so it's important that we know the absolute value in a no. I would hate for someone to say yes to me if they really didn't mean it.

I never want that. It's important to respect and embrace someone who is strong enough to say no. Kudos to someone who knows their heart is not in it. And it's absolutely possible to say no in the most loving way.

So this is how I have created my job from the ground up. I serve the best that I can, to the best of my ability with the right intentions. I put strong foundations in place and understand that we're forever growing. There will be growth spurts and times when we have the opportunity to pause and catch up.

At times, you say a yes when your heart is in, but you may not have the full knowledge of how to do it. You still need to say the yes to energise and equip yourself with the knowledge, and believe me, a person with a passion to serve their heart's desires is an absolute guarantee for success in my book.

So that's my story and my tips for creating the perfect job, for you, from the ground up. It starts with you. It starts with the seedling of an idea. It's where you will create the most amazing life for yourself that will bring harmony between life, work and your own success.

So tell me, what is your definition of success?

KAREN McDERMOTT

Karen is an award-winning publisher, author, TEDx speaker and advanced law of attraction practitioner.

Author of numerous books across many genres – fiction, motivational, children's and journals – she chooses to lead the way in her authorship, generously sharing her philosophies through her writing.

Karen is also a sought-after speaker who shares her knowledge and wisdom on building publishing empires, establishing yourself as a successful author-publisher and book writing.

Having built a highly successful publishing business from scratch, signing major authors, writing over thirty books herself and establishing her own credible brand in the market, Karen has developed strategies and techniques based on tapping into the power of knowing to create your dreams.

Karen is a gifted teacher who inspires others to make magic happen in their lives through her seven life principles that have been integral in her success.

Websites:
serenitypress.org
kmdbooks.com
mmhpress.com

THE POWER OF CONNECTION

Leezá Carlone Steindorf

One of the greatest gifts women have is that of connecting – to the life force, to ourselves, to others. Somewhere deep down, or in a whisp of memory, you know that intangible yet real experience of feeling tethered to the ground when standing under a tree, of feeling fierce when protecting a child, of feeling larger than yourself when you untangle from your thoughts and give yourself fully to the dance, to the garden, to the touch of your lover. We feel another's heart when emotions are shared or a child, not even our own, shares their longing for something just out of reach.

The spirit we bring as women to our world, our relationships, and our profession is essential, insightful, impactful. Yet, all too often, we listen to the voices of others to measure ourselves, to find our value. We ignore the deep knowing of our connection with all beings and our longing to help others connect as well.

Our Indigenous ancestors teach us the equal value of all things, even as each element has its differing impact on and place among the whole. The reason the web of life has functioned well over the millennia is thanks to the integrated dance of all beings and the essential order of all things. Yet, as soon as the thinking mind of humankind enters the mix, that order shifts to one of inequality and domination; well, unequal in some perspectives.

What would you say is more valuable, the delicate butterfly tiptoeing on the clover or the massive buffalo grazing nearby? Is the tiny ant carrying the pungent sage leaf more important than the powerful eagle soaring high above the desert floor? Are we humans more vital to life than the fish, the birds, the rivers or trees? In nature there is no hierarchy of value. All beings have their place and importance.

The notion that some living beings are better or worse than others is simply an illusion, a self-created and mass-perpetuated belief. This concept is destructively flawed. We humans have taken on as a fundamental truth the fallacy that there are number-one beings and number-two beings. It is a lie. There is no hierarchy in the value of beings, of any gender, age, creed or colour. Appropriately expressed in German, the name for equality is *gleichwertig* – of equal value.

Good to know, yet where does that get us?

Decades of intense study, led [1]primatologist Frans de Waal to conclude that masculine and feminine is, indeed, not clearly binary; it represents a spectrum. The range of respective gender traits are, more or less, pronounced toward masculine or feminine, depending both on the gender and the make-up of the individual. So, masculine and feminine are definitely distinct, yet not as a linear, hardwired, immovable series of points on a rigid grid for any person or gender. This is important to note. We move fluidly

---

1) *Different: Gender Through the Eyes of a Primatologist*, Frans de Wall, W. W. Norton & Company, 5 April 2022.

and flexibly within a personal range along that spectrum.

As such, discerning who we are as individuals within the gender we most strongly express is key to optimally unfolding our potential. Each gender has its unique obvious strengths and its quieter attributes. And as De Waal reminds us, 'Different doesn't mean better or worse.' Different means different, and that diversity is a very good thing.

Recently, I was asked, 'What is the biggest mistake that women make in business? Is it financial, strategic or maybe in decision-making?' My answer is none of those. Women's greatest mistake is trying to be like men. This is not meant to be snarky. Men do being men pretty well, yet women all too often struggle at being women. There are reams of historical, social, political and personal reasons for that struggle. Fundamentally, however, we are steeped in the illusion that, as women, we are in the number-two position. We believe that we have to work hard or change our nature in order to achieve, or deserve even, the number-one position.

The paradox is that we still seek, through those same historical, social and political structures, the permission to step into that top position, to find the freedom to finally be fully and freely who we are. We may have to continue working within our society's mental constructs, and have to deal with the resulting human dynamics. However, seeking sustainable change within the confines of that construct is incremental at best and often inefficient and impotent.

Here is a newsflash: there is no number-one or number-two group of humans. Period.

The radical transformation that allows us to live from that truth of equal value can only come from within ourselves. And that only happens when we stand fully in the unfiltered knowing of the depth, breadth and beauty of our gifts as individuals, as women, as humans.

We women are connected to the pulse of life. Our Indigenous elders remind us that women are the givers of life. Owning that gift of connection to life is our power. When we are aware of that strength of the feminine and are intentional with our connecting, we are undaunted. It is truly that simple.

Easier said than done, you say. Maybe, maybe not.

So, what does such a radical choice – to own the strength of our feminine gift of connection – look like in the business world? It demands us to be brutally true to our feminine self, in all of our unique and magnificent complexity. It takes courage, intention and practise in orienting first internally. When we are centred in our core self, we can then sovereignly focus on the external.

For example, one of my coaching clients, Elizabeth, is a brilliant senior executive in a large, male-dominated tech design firm. Elizabeth consistently leads her team to blaze through one goal after another. In just half the time set, her team alone has achieved the strategic planning goals assigned to their entire division. In short, she rocks as a leader.

In our last session, when she shared this amazing accomplishment, I acknowledged her for the finesse, skill and support she has brought forth to help her team to deliver such hardcore results so rapidly. As I said this, she looked at me with sincere surprise on her face. 'Well, it's not me! I've not done much. I'm just super lucky to have such an amazing team. They're the ones that have gotten us this far.' She is humble, yes. But she is also genuinely clueless.

'Indeed,' I said, 'they are ultimate professionals and whip-smart experts. Yet a group of highly skilled specialists does not automatically make a winning team. It takes leadership to facilitate those gifts so they can work together in a cohesive whole, negotiate the behavioural nuances and dissolve the inevitable tensions in order to create such amazing success. Good leadership magnifies the best in people and keeps people and projects aligned. A good leader generates a stellar team. *That* is what you have done.'

'Huh,' she said, looking perplexed. A long silence ensued. 'I hadn't thought about it that way.'

Mind you, this is a top executive in her field, highly experienced and nobody's fool. She just does not associate the tremendous success she helps generate daily with her own personal value. And sadly, she is not the exception. Most of the female leaders I work with are unaware of the incredible value they bring to the table. Elizabeth operates at high capacity without awareness of her deep worth, her own strength and her natural connection – to the life force, to herself and to others. Nor does she realise that she naturally engages those key elements of leadership to help her people reach their full potential and achieve such powerful results.

Part of the problem, in a practical sense, is that the word 'success' has been hijacked. Success is not something we achieve. It is our state of being, sourced in who we innately are. Although we strive hard to become 'better', there is nowhere for us to 'get to'. We already are who we most want to be, if we would just give ourselves permission to be so. Success is not a matter of doing more; it is a matter of being more of who you are.

If you dream of living a certain lifestyle, of mastering particular skills, of achieving intriguing goals, it is because those possibilities tickle at your consciousness from within, from the unseen part of yourself, urging you to manifest them. All of the dreams and possibilities that you are drawn to reside within you. The genesis of your success is who you are. It starts within and then manifests outward.

Recently, I finished a sales document that I had been working on for some time. Feeling relieved, I was finally pleased with the outcome as marketing materials are not my thing. I then started an email to send my shiny new info to the HR director of a venerable, multinational investment corporation in Boston, USA. Through coaching some of their leaders, I knew that they are eager to shift their corporate culture. Their company is based on solid values, yet, being in a male-dominated industry, there is ample repression of and discrimination toward women.

So, I had set my intention to facilitate for them the *CORE of Female Leadership*, sure that when their cohort of women leaders gain more clarity, discover their value and trust their voice, they will generate throughout the organisation the transformation so desperately needed.

Literally the second I started writing my greeting, an email pops into my inbox. It was from that very HR director. He asked me for the precise information on 'that women's program of yours' that I had just captured in the updated one-sheet. (Note: I hadn't communicated with him in over a month.)

Some would say that such timing is a coincidence, serendipity or even chance. I don't think so. That kind of synchronicity is no accident. It spins off from a level of connection with others that can be honed, even when wearing our business hat. When we lean into that strongest feminine gift of ours – connection – when we anchor in our value, things begin to align. It is not magic; it is the power of the feminine.

The key is to trust yourself. It's imperative.

What does the curious timing of receiving a request for the very information I was in the process of sending have to do with connection and thriving your business? Because just as there are no number-one and number-two humans, there is also no such thing as luck. There's no accidental success, no unintended progress, no 'oopsy' achievement. You are the constant.

Every action you take, large and small, takes place within a matrix of all thoughts and actions. Whether we know it, or not, we are a part of that system. All the thoughts, actions and way of being of the other leaders, entrepreneurs and business owners around you, who are committed to their own purpose and path, contribute intangibly to the thoughts you have and the decisions you make. There is no isolated energy in this vast field of life. We are never operating alone. We are connected, always. When we become aware of that connection, as subtle as it can be, and trust it, we can then utilise connection intentionally and impactfully.

Quantum physics has named this space the morphogenetic field. But without getting way far out there, suffice to say that there is a river of creative energy that we are each, and always, part of an unseen dynamic, a force working through us, with us and for us. Tuning into, trusting and engaging that creative energy as an active partner in who we are and what we do takes doing business and living life to a whole new level.

Women have unique access to that river of energy, to the inner voice, the quiet and expanded awareness of ideas, people and tangible projects. The sad truth is, however, that we have been systematically trained to doubt, discount and disown our relationship with that part of ourselves – our very core that generates creativity, sureness and ease.

As a child I was often told, 'You don't know what you're talking about.' Not necessarily demeaning words, but the impact on me was devastating. I grew up with very authoritarian parents who unintentionally helped solidify a deeply negative brick-and-mortar view of myself. Highly educated and well-meaning, they lived by strong values. Still, their constant messaging minimised my sense of self-worth and landed me in adulthood with zero self-esteem driven by immense pressure to perform at high capacity.

As a result, I spent my younger years in constant conflict with myself. I felt a critical urgency to accomplish excellence, yet was without any belief in myself or my abilities to do so.

Years later, in a conversation with a dear mentor, I felt a mental sizzle and spark when I recognised how ludicrous was the belief I had been holding as a holy truth that I did not know what I was talking about. If I'm the one talking, *of course* I know what I'm talking about! *Duh.* I may not be saying things the listener agrees with or understands. Still, *I always know* precisely what I am talking about. Sounds odd, but that was a revelation for me, and the shift was profound. I could finally feel the validity of my own inner voice. I experienced for the first time a confidence in myself, an untainted sureness of my own thoughts and words that I now lean into and rely on completely. That access had always been there, it was not new, yet I had been taught to believe I had no clue. I disowned my connection and concluded I was not of value.

If not hindered, women seem to be more easily aware of that deep connection to self and to all things. I believe that is because the feminine is non-linear in nature. Like the circles we women generate in all aspects of our lives – children's playgroups, girls' nights out, bridal showers, knitting circles, corporate focus groups – we naturally live from the centre of ourselves outward. We have accessed and celebrated over the millennia this connection to the life force, to self, to one another. It is in our nature. When we are aware that we are connected, we operate with more clarity, ease and joy in whatever we do.

Working over many years with men and women, business owners and corporate executives in over thirty-five cultures, it has become crystal clear that, for whatever reason, this natural way of knowing, of being, comes more easily to women. It has also become crystal clear that, globally, women are systematically discounted and discouraged from trusting this natural feminine internal operating system.

With the critical juncture this world is at right now, it is high time that we fully trust our innate femininity and our connectivity to all that is. Download that system, update it and let it run as it was designed to.

Internal & external orientation

Can it possibly be so easy to connect within, even though we have been bullied and bulldozed to disbelieve our own selves? Indeed, it is. We can easily sync with the part of ourselves that is connected with the life force because it is who we are. We have had to make an effort to disconnect; we just forgot we did so as it happened so early in our lives. We can rediscover our value and thrive in business by connecting with ourselves, our colleagues and our clients. We must simply be intentional about where we place our focus, internally or externally, then use that orientation as our most reliable GPS.

Whatever we do, we can either orient from within – experiencing our inner world, feelings and thoughts and basing our choices and actions on that reality – or we can orient from without – viewing ourselves and situations from another's perspective, an external viewpoint, and base our decisions on that stance. For most of our day, in most conversations and relationships, we toggle between the two orientations mostly without awareness that we are doing so. Bringing the process into our awareness, making the shift from internal to external orientation intentional, being conscious of where our perspective and thought processes are based, within or without, is the most powerful tool a leader can cultivate.

At the start, as infants and small children, we had no other orientation – our world began within, and we saw and felt only from an internal orientation. The world was a heightened experience of our inner senses and perceptions. The ability to view ourselves and our world from an external viewpoint comes much later in human development. So, internal orientation is natural to us. It is where we all started. And it is the realm of connection and a sense of rightness, of personal value.

Sadly, however, we have become so far removed from our own internal experience that most of us do not even know how we feel at any given moment. In distancing ourselves from our source, we have come to believe in the fallacy we were taught and that society as a whole has swallowed. We have concluded that there is a hierarchy of value, a superiority of certain beings and an inferiority of others. That belief is what shackles our ability to navigate this world, and our very own path, with a sense of ease and in a way that serves our personal highest good.

Yet, we can return to the ease of feeling connected. Start by recognising and owning your own value, by orienting within, anchoring yourself to the home base of inner connection. From there, you can accomplish whatever you put your focus on.

As you are reading this, observe from within your own mind's eye and heart space. What are you feeling? What are you sensing? What are you thinking? Take stock of your internal landscape, view your experience from this uniquely personal internal lens. From within, notice what is going on right now around you – the people, activities, sights and sounds. Take just a moment from reading this and experience this moment from deep within.

Now, shift your awareness to an external perspective. Orient without and become the observer of you – of where you are sitting, of what you are thinking or feeling, perhaps as another may perceive you.

Notice how the experience of observing yourself and your

world from a perspective outside of yourself differs from anchoring within and being internally oriented. Notice if you shifted completely away from any sense of being connected to yourself while you were observing and externally oriented.

Now, see if you can tether yourself to your internal anchor while you step outside of that personal lens to see what others may be seeing. Can you hold awareness from both perspectives? This is not easy, so do not get disheartened if you're not yet able to. Just know that it is possible to perceive your external surroundings and the experience of others without losing connection with yourself or your experience. This is how we maintain awareness of our own value while going about our business and life, by remaining connected with ourselves.

It is usually in the external orientation, by hooking ourselves into others' perspectives, that we begin to judge ourselves, devalue what we offer and diminish our own worth. We are not trained to see the value of ourselves while also seeing the value of others. Of course, that is both possible and also optimal.

It just takes practising internal orientation. From that solid stance, you strengthen your sense of worth without the temptation of comparing yourself to others.

When you can stay connected with yourself and still grasp what others are doing or feeling from their perspective, you are able to connect with them in a deeper, more meaningful way without losing yourself. From that place, you can value both yourself and the other. With that practise, from that space, you can best serve your clients. You can see more clearly, provide more accurate guidance and offer more targeted resources and support.

The power of connection in four simple steps

Understanding the techniques to build both powerful and

sustainable connections is easier than you think. Here are steps to help you access the power of connection:

Connect first with yourself
Get quiet, centre and become aware of your inner landscape. Feel rooted and at ease in the value of who you are.

Remaining anchored within yourself
Become aware of what is around you. Slowly shift your focus to your client, to what they are saying, experiencing and asking for.

Communicate
Discuss what you have observed about them and their circumstances, and from your internal tether, share how you would like to support them. Let them feel the connection between you both. Invite a conversation about the 'we' aspect instead of the 'I' in your business relationship.

Assist
Help your client connect to themselves, to orient both internally and externally, as you have now learned to do. Help them to see how they're operating; which actions and behaviours are useful to them, and which are not, to achieve their goals. Speak to the connection between the two of you and of your commitment to supporting them, walking with them and helping them achieve what they set as an intention. Help them make contact with their own power and acknowledge their own worth. Help them clarify their wishes, ideas, resources and the opportunities around them. Help them identify people that will uplift them, value them, move them forward and strategically strengthen their ability to manifest their objectives.

When you come home to your own value, when you feel the connection to that unseen force, to yourself and all that is around you, much stress and tension falls away. You can operate with more ease and calm. When you connect with your whole self, you can feel the strength of the ever-present unseen force. By whatever name, that strong current of support unfolds for us, and with us, the way forward. Even as we invest ourselves in moving mountains, mastering details and closing deals, we can listen quietly within.

Practise connecting. Feel your value. Build a partnership with this unseen guide within, feel into and rely on it. You will learn to navigate encounters, opportunities and ideas with clarity, curiosity and a light sense of freedom.

When we operate from this natural centre of connection within ourselves, we are home. From there, we can connect with others more easily and authentically. And when we come to truly appreciate our innate value, we discover that living and working can be a creative, impactful and outlandishly good experience.

LEEZÁ CARLONE STEINDORF

As a global thought leader, consultant and leadership coach for corporations, executives and state representatives for over twenty years in more than thirty-five countries, Leezá helps individuals and organisations gain clarity amid confusion, simplify structures out of complexity and transform tension into ease and confidence. Leezá specializes in helping women break through limiting beliefs, shatter their own internal glass ceiling and thrive.

Leezá is an executive coach for Forbes Coaches Council, a Canfield Success Trainer, former Tony Robbins Results Coach and host of the public TV show *Live With Leezá*. Her certifications include ICF Executive and Life Coach, Trainer and Group Facilitator, Mediator and NonViolent Communication Trainer. She holds a degree in business management and her

CORE Success™ trainings are internationally acclaimed and accredited.

You are invited to contact: leezá@coresuccess.com

'Leezá is like a laser through the fog, bright and illuminating.'
US Senator Diane Allen, author of the Diane B. Allen Equal Pay Act

MARKET DEVELOPMENT

Linda Fisk

As Sushil cleared her throat, trying to regain her composure, she could feel a single bead of sweat run down her neck as her stomach tightened. She could see her hands trembling slightly as blood rushed to her face, making her blush uncomfortably. She gripped the podium with both hands, ready to respond to the flurry of thinly veiled accusations and sharply directed comments from her board of directors.

Sushil had just reported her company's dismal quarterly performance, after a long period of stagnant sales and disappointed financial results, and her plans to help drive a rebound in the next quarter.

Sushil was a frustrated founder, who hit a growth plateau, and was in the unenviable position of having to report to the board the disappointing performance of the past quarter, which only compounded the lacklustre results of the past year. Sushil's company seemed to be stalling, and she had not presented a plan that engendered any sense of confidence from the board.

Testing different growth strategies had slowed and goals weren't being met. These two factors led to a stagnant user growth chart and a company that seemed to have peaked much earlier than the financial forecast had outlined.

Can you relate?

As a business founder, you will undoubtedly find yourself forced to make countless decisions that, collectively, will determine the overall success of your company. These decisions may feel small when they involve things like who to hire and when, but they will almost certainly feel more consequential when they involve things like optimising sales models, pricing models and high-impact growth strategies.

And one of the most important series of decisions you will make is how to seamlessly move between the early startup phase of your business to a well-managed stage of exponential growth. As businesses enter the growth phase, crafting a carefully considered market development strategy helps to identify and develop new opportunities to sell current products or services into new, unexplored markets. In an effort to increase sales, a savvy business owner should consider how best to position their products or services to a widening segment of consumers.

Strategies to fuel business growth

According to Igor Ansoff, the father of strategic management, there are only four main strategies to fuel meaningful business growth: diversification strategy, market penetration strategy, product development strategy and market development strategy. The market development strategy is a business growth strategy that involves selling existing products or services into new markets, often through repositioning those products and services.

The market development strategy allows a business to leverage existing products and take them to a different market – and there are a couple of different approaches to consider:

- Catering to a different customer segment or target demographic.
- Entering a new domestic market (regional expansion).
- Entering into a foreign market (international expansion).

For example, Lululemon management made a decision to aggressively expand into the Asia-Pacific market to sell its already very popular athleisure products. While building an advertising and logistics infrastructure in a foreign market inherently presents risks, it's less risky because Lululemon is selling a proven product with a successful track record.

Your strategy and your choice

Before you expand into a new domestic or foreign market or cater to a different audience segment (perhaps by positioning your product for new uses), it's important to identify what your biggest development opportunities are. This can help you determine which opportunities may be the most successful and provide you with valuable insight to help you reach your goals.

Here are a few of the considerations and choices available to you:

Same area, different customers

As the name suggests, in this strategy you would choose to target new customer segments in the same existing market where your products or services are already selling. For example, if a chewing gum 'Fresh and Juicy' was targeted for teenagers and kids, then with careful repositioning of the product and a smart promotional plan, the same chewing gum could be targeted to adults as well.

In this case, how you position the product or service is the key to success.

Different area, same customers

In this strategy, you would choose to expand to a different geographic area, but consistently target the same customer profile. For example, if a contemporary clothing line targeting professional working women 'Smart and Snappy' is only available in New York, then, using this strategy, the clothing line could target the same professional working women in California under the 'Smart and Snappy' label.

If you choose to pursue this strategy, take care that when changing geography, factors associated with the target audience's preferences and lifestyles have been taken into consideration. For example, the most popular moisturiser sold in Sweden, formulated to be especially effective in a cold and dry climate, may not have the same market reaction in Nigeria. In this case, specific changes would have to be made to the existing strategy to fit the new market – and it may be appropriate to look for new uses of the existing product in the new Nigerian market.

Different area, different customers

If you choose this strategy, you are willing to take a greater risk to grow and scale your business. As the name suggests, the product remains the same, but the market area is different, and even the customers you are targeting are different. For example, a healthy food chain 'Simply Natural' that targets health-conscious customers in a particular geographical area decides to open a new store in a different location that targets the elderly population. Although it is possible that the healthy food chain may be a success targeting the over-sixty-five senior population, there is also a significant risk of failure.

Benefits of a market development strategy

As a business owner begins to enter a period of significant growth or are ready to scale their business, creating a market development strategy can be pivotal, because it can help reach a wider audience of potential customers and grow the business. Creating a carefully considered, strategic market development strategy can also help you:

- Improve the quality of your products or services.
- Acquire new customers.
- Upsell current customers.
- Develop new products or services.
- Increase revenue margins.
- Build organisational resilience.
- Support long-term company growth.
- Generate more leads and sales.
- Provide more value to customers.
- Increase brand awareness.
- Decrease your production cost per unit.

While each business may take a slightly different approach to create a market development strategy that aligns with their industry, their business goals and the specific products or services they are offering, there are some basic steps you can take to get started.

Different paths to the same summit

A market development strategy involves gaining a larger percentage of the total serviceable market – and you can do that by: 1) identifying, targeting and attracting new customers to purchase your products or services, or 2) you can boost sales by convincing your current customers to use your products or services in new ways.

For example, if your company has traditionally targeted women, you may now try to consider the needs of men. Consider the fact that some of the most popular cosmetics and skin product brands, who have traditionally only targeted women, have been expanding their market by specifically targeting men for the past two decades. You can consider new customer opportunities by identifying prospects in different parts of the country, or even other countries. You can also identify new customer segments based on consumers' personality traits, values or interests. It may also involve dividing the market into segments based on people's lifestyles.

The ideal method of a market development strategy will look different for every business, so you should think about what approach best suits your unique business operation and the type of products or services you offer.

Suggest new uses for your existing products or services
Discovering new uses for your product enables you to promote to new customers and expand into new markets. Humans are curious creatures that are exceptional at being creative, resourceful and improvising solutions, so how you think your product is being used may not be entirely correct. Surveying and interviewing your customers can reveal innovative ways that people are using your product to solve their problems. In turn, this can give you fresh ideas about how to market and who to market to.

Geographic expansion to find new customers
If your product has started small, expansion into new national or international areas might be the next phase of your market

development. If identifying and developing new market segments is your preferred strategy, careful consideration should be made around:

- Whether you have enough resources to expand into a new market.
- Whether your product will be ultimately successful in this new market.
- Whether the market is going to be valuable enough to put the resources, budget and effort into expanding in this direction.
- Whether the potential new market is already too saturated, or whether you can gain market share and stay competitive.

Customer expansion to win new audience segments
A good first step to identify and develop new market segments for your current products or services is to target non-buying customers in currently targeted audiences. Clearly identify who you are targeting, and then determine: 1) who are your loyal, consistent customers, 2) who are your occasional buyers, and 3) who has never purchased from you and why?

One of the best examples of this strategy is the famous Harry Potter books. The author, J K Rowling, initially launched the books for kids, but after the massive success of the series, she introduced the books with reworked art on the cover page that appealed uniquely to adults – the graphics were more serious and the characters more mature. Although the plot was the same, the makeover of the books was targeted to the adult population. She also introduced a unique series of books for teenagers in which the book cover was reworked to appeal to teens although the plot was kept precisely the same.

Begin at the beginning with market research

Before starting the market development, a business should think about their current and prospective customer. The primary question in this stage is to answer who your customer is. Customers can be differentiated on their age, gender, status, parental status, investments, profession and many other factors. Identifying – and describing in explicit detail – who you're targeting for your products and services will help your business plan your market development strategies.

In fact, market development can be considered a two-step process, beginning with market research. By initiating a segmentation analysis, which analyses a small slice of the overall potential market, you can determine which audience segments are worth pursuing. You can segment a market along the lines of demographic, geographic, psychographic, product-benefit specifications and more.

To conduct thorough market research related to your customers and products, address questions like what does the financial profile of the target audience look like, what are the income levels of the target audience, what are the competitor products used by the target audience, why are the customers using the competitor products and more.

Apart from focusing on the detailed profile of prospective customers, market research should also be conducted on your competitors as well. Understanding how many competitors you face, where they are located, which products or services are they offering, the pricing structure of competitive products, their performance histories and their strengths and weaknesses are just a few of the factors to consider.

Proper market research will help to build a healthy market development plan. Analysing the buying habits of people, understanding their interests and the effect of various factors which influence the buying behaviour of the customer like climate, geography, political factors, sociological factors, etc. following what products the customer is currently using and why is a most crucial part of market research.

Once the analysis and market research are completed, you will have a good idea about the growth potential for your product or service in this current market. If the market plan is lucrative and will be able to get decent profits, then you can comfortably enter the market.

There is always going to be some risk in venturing into a new market, and your ability to accept that level of risk will determine whether you want to enter the market or not. If you do not introduce even the slightest chance of failure, then entering a new market will be suitable for your product or service. But, if you're comfortable with some amount of risk, then the market is worth pursuing.

Once you have determined which market segments are worth pursuing, the second step of market development involves creating clear positioning for your product or service, to highlight your unique value in the marketplace, and then creating a promotional strategy to penetrate the new market.

The power of positioning

Competition is fierce, no matter which business you're in. Finding ways to differentiate yourself from other companies in your space – such as offering better support, more competitive pricing, or extra features that are in demand and not offered by your competitors – can entice customers to switch over to your product. Make your product more appealing to gain more market share from your competitors' customers.

When it comes to positioning your product or service in the marketplace, you have to intentionally choose from three distinct positions: you will either compete on the high end, the low end or in the middle. In other words, you either offer a high-end product or service, a low-cost solution or you try to straddle the middle and be all things to all people. You may need to consider what has to change to bring about a shift in your market position. To survive and thrive, you'll need to either: 1) scale down into a niche you can defend, 2) dominate the middle and scale up, or 3) compete at the top of the market with potentially bigger competitors.

So, it's critical to think about a few aspects before choosing a positioning strategy. Answering a few questions can help you map out the path forward. The following are a few points to be considered:

- Target customers: Are the target customers properly identified, profiled and described? What are their expectations? What are they currently using in terms of products or services? How does the competitor satisfy the needs of the customer? Why would customers be loyal to a competitor?
- Profitability: Would a market development strategy be profitable? What are the expected returns from this strategy, and more importantly, when can the profits be expected?
- Current products: Is there a need to introduce a modified product, which would be a different version of the existing product? Will it satisfy the demand in the market and fulfil the needs of customers?
- New products: What is the cost and the time line of adding new products in the market? When will the company expect the return on investment? Or is launching a new product the only

option available? Will it be more successful than the strategy of modified products?

The benefits of your product or service should be explained in such a way that it convinces the new target segment to try your product or service, but at the same time, does not discourage your existing customers from future purchases.

Here's a quick case study of a young startup that deployed a market development strategy effectively and became a worldwide household name.

A new social media platform that was designed exclusively for Harvard University began to gain traction on campus. As the platform grows, the founders that developed the social media platform realise there's an opportunity to reach users from other colleges and universities. The company updates its account policies to allow anyone who is a college student to register. The social media platform gradually grows as more students tell their friends at different schools about the platform. After the social media platform successfully expands to other colleges and universities, the company allows people who aren't students to register for the platform.

They research this new customer segment and make some slight changes to their social media platform to make it more inclusive. Then they develop a marketing plan to help them introduce their social media platform to new users. By slowly expanding from one target audience to the next, the company is able to gradually adjust their platform to meet the needs of different customers. This helps them improve the quality of their product, provide more value to existing users and attract new users. I'm sure by now you can guess the name of this company – Facebook!

In 2004, backed by a few thousand dollars from its co-founders,

Facebook launched as a small, minimalist social networking site limited to Harvard undergraduates. And now Facebook's market cap is valued at $502 billion with an enterprise value of $490 billion!

Shout it from the rooftop

Once you're clear on your positioning, a detailed marketing and promotional plan is needed to introduce and promote your product to the new target market. This plan should outline all the unique audience segments you are targeting, the key messaging that you're going to use by audience, the specific marketing channels and platforms and the primary audience touchpoints. Across all marketing channels and platforms, you should consider whether you are:

- Targeting new customers in your existing market.
- Seeking to sell into new markets.
- Positioning your product or service for new uses.

Once you have allocated the necessary resources, determined who you are specifically targeting and identified all of the relevant customer touchpoints, it's time to develop a plan to launch your new product or service into a new market or introduce an existing product to new customers. This can help you build brand awareness and generate demand. Some marketing channels and opportunities you may consider developing a strategic plan for include:

- Email marketing.
- Social media marketing.
- Local marketing.

- Digital content and blog posts.
- Streaming television.
- Billboards and event advertising.
- Print advertisements.
- Radio and television ads.

You can revisit the research you've compiled about your target audience to determine which marketing channels they use the most. Establish KPIs for your campaign, such as the number of people reached or the number of clicks back to your website. Then track these KPIs throughout the campaign to identify areas for improvement and assess your progress.

With the help of digital marketing, promotional campaigns can be targeted explicitly to the selected audiences so that the messaging does not reach an unwanted audience causing waste of resources. Similarly, if the target market is not defined correctly, then there is a possibility of the market development process failing to reach the most profitable and productive audience segments.

For example, you may decide to engage in a very targeted direct email campaign, combined with very prescriptive social media outreach, based on the specific audience segment you want to reach. If you have defined your audience well, through geographic, psychographic, demographic profiling as well as past purchasing behaviour, you can reduce your marketing budget while increasing your impact.

Free trials, targeted content marketing, advertising and experimenting with pricing strategies can be a useful part of your marketing development strategy, as they can encourage non-customers in your existing market to become customers.

For example, Slack began offering a free service that was incredibly useful. Teams who saw the value of the free service would get the better options with a paid version of the platform – to a tune of a 30% conversion rate (free to paid). So Slack is free to use at first, but as a team or organisation grows, it costs more. In fact, Slack's app store contains different integrations, bots, apps and more – and some are free, others are premium. The B2B marketplace inside of Slack is perhaps why it's valuation is unicorn-like, at $2.8 billion. As an online service for business collaboration, this is one of best places to look at marketplace.

To increase your likelihood of success, openly communicate with your team about your goals, progress and action steps. Provide key team members with your overarching marketing campaign and sales plan to ensure they understand what tasks they're responsible for and how you plan to measure success. Provide regular status updates about the launch time line, upcoming tasks and deadlines to help your team stay organised and on track.

Let's check in on Sushil again.

After that nerve-racking board meeting, Sushil adopted a carefully considered market development strategy that helped her identify and develop new opportunities to sell the company's current products or services into new, unexplored markets. She worked with her team to consider how best to position their products or services to a widening segment of consumers, by answering the following questions:

- Is the strategy profitable? If so, what is the likely return on investment?
- Will the business need to introduce modified products?
- Will the business need to introduce new products?
- Has the business researched their target consumers extensively enough?

Satisfied that the company was ready to embark on a new market development strategy, Sushil and her team developed specific, measurable, achievable, relevant and time-based goals for the key areas of her business, including:

- Sales.
- Net profit.
- Employees.
- Products.
- Customers or users.
- Geographic locations.

Once Sushil expanded into her carefully considered new market, she began tracking her results to ensure that her company met the stated goals and satisfied their new customers. She started collecting sales data to assess how successful her company's launch was and began assessing whether she could meet her projections. She met with her team regularly to identify areas for improvement and to optimise the company's launch campaign to help them reach their goals.

Sushil's company is a fintech SaaS company that offers payment processing software and APIs for ecommerce websites and mobile apps. It also offers services like fraudulent transaction blocker, invoicing, point-of-sale service and more. After Sushil crafted her market development strategy, carefully positioning the company's products and services, and launched her promotional campaign, she saw immediate gains, breaking out of the stagnant sales plateau she had been struggling with for the past two years.

Millions of companies of all sizes – from startups to Fortune 500s – now use Sushil's software and APIs to accept payments, send payouts and manage their businesses online. Sushil now makes moving money as simple, borderless and programmable as the rest of the internet. And her team has expanded to key office locations around the world, processing billions of dollars each year. The current value of Sushil's company is $9.5 billion, and it received investments from some of the top venture capital firms in the world.

Are you next?

LINDA FISK

Linda Fisk is a multi-award-winning leader, keynote speaker, bestselling author and university professor dedicated to amplifying and extending the success of other high-calibre business leaders. She is the founder and CEO of LeadHERship Global, a community of unstoppable women enhancing their leadership blueprint and embracing their power to be the best version of themselves – in work and life. In LeadHERship Global, Linda supports and guides ambitious, creative women to move in the direction of their purpose, their mission and their dreams with powerful connections, critical support, practical tools and valuable resources to show up, speak up and step up in their careers and personal lives.

Prior to her role in LeadHERship Global, Linda was the CEO

of Collective 54, successfully launching, growing and scaling that firm after serving as the global head of brand marketing, public relations and communications at Susan G. Komen. Linda forged a earlier career as an entrepreneurial and forward-thinking marketing executive on the cutting edge of brand marketing. When Linda served as the global head of marketing for YPO, she developed her passion for bringing inspiring leaders together to create opportunity, discover possibility and solve problems.

Linda has a PhD and MA in clinical psychology and has written extensively on the subjects of social comparison, depression and anxiety, subjective wellbeing and personality theory, with a focus on relating scientific research to commonly understood concepts. Currently, Linda is interested in the psychology of influence, persuasion and negotiation.

INSIGHTS INTO WHY CONSUMERS BUY FROM YOU

Naila Qazi

Every success comes with a backstory
Consumer behaviour refers to how and why individuals look for, buy, select, use and dispose of products and services. It encapsulates many issues, including motivation, decision-making, consumer attitudes, influences and perceptions.

Being raised in Chiniot, a small, rural town in Pakistan, came with its struggles. Being a girl raised by a lower-middle-class, conservative family in a country where the social and cultural values clashed meant gender equality felt far from possible. With little in terms of resources and a tough journey to keep myself in school, I had to earn my place. My upbringing fuelled me to make a different life for myself. I knew that, to achieve success, I had a fight on my hands. However, adversity can become your best friend if you know how to hold the power wisely.

According to the World Economic Forum's (WEF) [1] 2021 *Global Gender Gap Report,* the female labour force participation in Pakistan remains stuck at 22.6%, with women making up a mere 4.9% of senior business roles. Clear sex preferences, combined with religious, cultural and social factors, make advancing in the business world as a woman nearly impossible. This, coupled with the lack of female role models, made things even more difficult for me. Without diversity and representation, it was hard to see myself in roles that simply didn't take women into consideration. This is especially prevalent when it comes to corporate environments. Yet, strength comes from challenges, and this drove me to strive for more.

Instead of accepting the position society had deemed fit for a woman, I did everything I could to keep myself in school. Whether it was doing chores, fetching water or running around looking after my younger siblings, I did whatever was necessary to continue my education and growth. Unfortunately, I had to make double the effort that men did to get the opportunities they got without even trying. Yet, this didn't stop me from reaching for the stars – it only made inequality and sexism clear to me in a way that pushed me to better myself and ensure I could change these circumstances for the next generation.

Success amidst adversity

While I struggled to find opportunities when I was younger, I worked hard to gain every advantage I could. When I grew up, things changed. I got married, migrated to Australia and started a family. However, I continued to work hard and completed a master's degree at the University of Melbourne at the same time to further my career and constantly learn. After completing my MBA

---

1) weforum.org/reports/global-gender-gap-report-2021

in Sydney and running a few businesses, I embraced travelling and eventually migrated to Canada.

Following years in different countries like Pakistan, Australia and North America, my experience has given me a unique insight into the importance of a global mindset. As such, I value constant improvement and proving my worth by putting in the effort and contributing to all the companies I've been fortunate enough to work for. My foundations have been built on hard work and proving myself and have led to me becoming a global citizen who is passionate about education, inclusion and diversity.

The importance of understanding consumer behaviour

If you're an entrepreneur or a business owner, the importance of understanding consumer behaviour cannot be stressed enough. In fact, this is essential if you want to be successful in launching or advertising products and services. It's by understanding consumer behaviour that businesses can effectively market and sell their products and services. Understanding influences on buying behaviour also gives companies insight into influencing their target audience, becoming more competitive and maintaining a loyal group of customers.

Additionally, consumers now expect companies to better understand them. According to Salesforce, [2]66% of customers expect companies to understand their expectations and needs. If a company does not, this could result in wasted advertising dollars and consumers simply taking their business elsewhere by buying from competitors. Failure to understand consumer behaviour can directly affect sales, and ultimately, a business' success. In addition to marketing and sales, consumer behaviour analysis

---
2) salesforce.com/resources/articles/customer-expectations

is essential for predicting trends, consumer differentiation and even the development of products and services. Thus, successful organisations take advantage of consumer behaviour insights and use them to grow and thrive.

Factors that affect consumer behaviour

A myriad of factors affect buyer behaviour, whether it's in making purchases, being likely to repurchase products or even in deciding not to make a purchase. These range from external influences like culture, family, reference groups and marketing, to internal influences like motives, perceptions and emotions.

Situational factors

Situational factors are factors that are out of the consumer's control. One example of this is store layout. Everyone knows the all-too-familiar trope of being lost in a store and being unable to make your way out. This is no coincidence. Store layout and design are carefully considered and serve a purpose: to make consumers spend more money. Consider IKEA's store design, which takes customers through the entire store. Similarly, casinos usually don't have visible exit signs and are designed in a way that makes gamblers stay longer. Another example is store location. Starbucks has outlets every few blocks and in airports and department stores.

Personal factors

Aspects such as personality, age, occupation, financial status, values and stage in life are important factors that contribute to purchasing decisions. Interest and taste in products and services change based on age and what part of their life the consumer is in. For example, married vs. single people, parents vs. people without kids and those starting out in their careers vs. retired individuals all have different needs and would have differing purchases.

Another personal factor that affects purchasing decisions is one's lifestyle. Those with busy lives usually look for products and services that make their lives easier, while this is less important to those who are more constrained by money rather than time. For example, someone who is time constrained may buy more expensive products because they may save time. Multitasking products such as combination foundation and sunscreens and hair straighteners that dry hair at the same time are excellent examples of this. On the other hand, those who are more money constrained will give more weight to price than to convenience.

Occupation, income and financial situation also affect purchasing habits. For example, a business executive may have the money to buy an expensive personal computer, but the same can't be said for a college student who is struggling to pay their bills. Additionally, even the same category of a product would differ based on different circumstances. For example, two consumers may both need a pair of shoes, but based on their occupations and financial situation, one may buy off-brand shoes while another may spend money on designer shoes.

Personality traits also come into account since many consumers identify with brand personalities, which influence their buying decisions. Conversely, choosing a specific brand may be less about their personality and more about what they want to achieve. Buying may even be affected by others and their perception of the individual and the brand.

Social factors
Social factors include friends, family, other reference groups, social status and even social roles. These can all influence individuals

by exposing them to products and lifestyles or by establishing norms and rules that cannot be broken. This need to conform may inform buying behaviour. Likewise, social roles and social status can also lead individuals to conform to specific buying behaviour. For example, suburban parents usually choose mini-vans when it comes to car purchases, while high-powered executives may choose more flashy cars to signify their societal status.

Cultural factors

Cultural factors consist of a consumer's culture, subculture and even social class. Since culture informs individual behaviour and wants, it plays a significant role in purchasing habits. For example, different types of clothing are prevalent in different countries. Additionally, alcohol is a common purchase in Western countries, but not in the Middle East. Even social class plays a large role in purchasing habits since those in the upper class have certain brand preferences and are more likely to purchase luxury items.

Psychological factors

Psychological factors are an integral part of understanding consumer behaviour and purchase decisions. Motivation, learning, perception and memory are all essential factors that directly influence individuals' buying decisions.

Motivation drives consumers to act, but motivation differs depending on needs. For example, Maslow's Hierarchy of Needs dictates that more urgent needs must be satisfied before moving on to less pressing needs. Thus, basic needs such as sustenance and shelter are more important than esteem needs such as status and recognition.

Learning is yet another factor that affects buyers. Once individuals learn about a product, they change their behaviour. Cues and biases play a role in this, as do companies' attempts to inform consumers about their products and services. For example, this can be through taste tests, samples, test drives, sales reps and even brochures and information-focus advertisements.

Similarly, perception drives buying behaviour since consumers perceive information that they use to guide their purchasing habits. This depends on both physical stimuli and how it relates to the surrounding environment. Whether it's ambiance and music in a store, an especially aggressive salesperson or a product's looks, a consumer's perception will guide their actions.

In economics, there's a basic assumption that individuals are rational and act in their best interests. However, this is not always the case, especially regarding buying decisions. Whether it's impulse shopping or buying based on emotions, consumer responses and behaviours are not always logical and rational. Companies recognise this and use it to their advantage through emotion-based appeals, nostalgia marketing and more.

The consumer buying process

The buying process is complex and is influenced by a multitude of factors. Examining the buying process is confusing because it starts long before consumers officially start thinking of purchases. However, when looking at the bigger picture, marketers have come up with a five-stage system that encapsulates the consumer buying process. Fully understanding this process is essential despite it not always holding true or involving all the steps because it provides a frame of reference into the buying journey and how to influence it.

Purchase involvement & decision-making

The buying process should be viewed through the lens of purchase involvement and decision-making. This is because the process differs depending on the item and the consumer's need for it. For example, an individual may not think much about the brand of bottled water they're buying when they're thirsty but would spend a lot more time thinking about the home they're about to purchase. This is where purchase involvement comes in. The phrase refers to the level of interest in or concern about the purchase and the purchase process. It's important to note that purchase involvement doesn't depend on the product itself but on the consumer, how interested they are in the purchase and how important the purchase is to them.

Low-involvement consumer decisions

Low-involvement decisions don't require a lot of risks, aren't usually novel, and are thus, straightforward. In fact, these usually lead to a habit, especially when repeating purchases. While consumers do select the product they want and ensure it satisfies their needs, they don't spend more time or effort than is needed. For example, a consumer buying toothpaste may not go through all stages of the buying process. Instead of spending time contemplating their decision and looking at different brands and claims, they're more likely to purchase the toothpaste they've been using for years. The buying process is a routine and doesn't require a lot of time or consideration. Most low-involvement purchase decisions consist of routine products, products that are inexpensive and those that don't pose a risk to the consumer.

High-involvement consumer decisions

High-involvement decisions are much more important to the buyer and usually involve some level of risk. These decisions aren't as straightforward as buying toothpaste, chewing gum or trash bags.

They may include a variety of risks, including financial, psychological and social risks. To avoid negative consequences, consumers spend more time and energy when evaluating options and alternatives. Especially high-involvement cases, such as buying a house or car, involve an extended problem-solving process and may involve going through all the stages of the consumer buying process.

Limited problem-solving & limited decision-making

This falls somewhere between high-involvement and low-involvement decisions. In this case, the consumer usually has some knowledge about a good or service, such as pricing, features and other options. Thus, while they may do additional research, such as looking up product information online or asking for recommendations, they will come to a decision fairly quickly. Because of this previously existing information, the decision-making process and involvement are lowered. For example, if a consumer has previously purchased a sleeping bag and now needs a new one, they will already be familiar with the options, pricing and features. Thus, the decision-making process would not take as long as it may for someone who is purchasing a sleeping bag for the first time.

Stages in the consumer buying process

The following are the stages in the buying process. Not all of them are always utilised, and there's no strict order that must be followed. However, this framework is useful for contextualising how consumers make their purchases.

Problem recognition
The first step is the consumer realising that they have a need that must be met. This may be an internal realisation or it could be

triggered by external forces such as family and friends or marketing. For example, an individual may realise that they need a new cell phone. This could be due to their current phone acting up, because their friend or family member just purchased a new phone or because they saw an online advertisement for the latest iPhone. No matter how this realisation is triggered, the consumer has now recognised a problem and will act upon it.

Depending on the type of purchase, this could be one that is thought about in detail or one that's made almost immediately. For example, a low-involvement purchase won't be treated the same as a high-involvement purchase. If an individual is hungry and wants to order food, the decision-making process on this will be much simpler and quicker than buying a new car.

Information search

Having recognised the problem, the next step in the buying process is searching for information that would help consumers make the right purchasing decision. Before seeking information from external sources, consumers first use memories and past experiences to think about the decision. Once this is done, they move on to external sources, such as friends, family, advertisements, recommendations from professional organisations and going in-store and handling the item themselves.

The information-searching stage isn't always present for products that consumers are purchasing all the time, such as copy paper or milk. However, it's usually present when buying something for the first time or if it's a high-involvement decision like buying a luxury bag or wedding dress.

Alternative & product evaluation

While all consumers evaluate products and their alternatives in their own unique way, one thing is common in this process – narrowing down products and services to their attributes. From there, consumers look at the options they have narrowed down and look at the different attributes to assess which brand will satisfy their needs.

When consumers judge products, they usually have a minimum acceptance level in mind, prioritise some attributes over others, determine which ones cannot be compromised and then decide. It's important to remember that the attributes consumers are interested in differ from product to product. For example, when buying a car, they may look at attributes such as speed, safety and seating capacity. However, these attributes would be very different for a hotel, where a consumer may focus on location, amenities provided, cleanliness and price.

Selection & purchase decision
Once the selection is made, it's time to make other decisions related to the purchase, such as which retailer to buy from, whether there are any discounts available, etc. With low-involvement purchases, consumers usually skip many stages and jump directly from problem recognition to selection and purchase of a product or service. It's important to note that the purchase decision isn't always positive – sometimes, consumers decide not to buy a product in order to save money or may opt for another product altogether.

Post-purchase behaviour & processes
The buying process isn't over once the purchase is made. Post-purchase behaviour is an essential part of the process and consists of post-purchase actions, satisfaction and more. When consumers aren't satisfied with the product they end up choosing and purchasing, they face post-purchase dissonance or buyer's remorse.

This is usually the case with high-involvement products that are usually novel or rare and more expensive.

It's in a business' best interest to ensure post-purchase satisfaction. If not, this may result in returning the product, abandoning it and the brand or complaining to others about it. If companies keep their customers satisfied, they're likely to benefit from glowing recommendations and customer satisfaction. Businesses try to combat buyer's remorse by offering money-back guarantees, warranties and customer service help. Additionally, they try to do this by setting expectations. This is because meeting expectations only satisfies the consumer. Exceeding expectations will result in much more satisfaction and may even delight. For example, if a repairman tells a consumer it will take four days to fix an item, and they do it in two days instead, the customer is much more satisfied than if it had taken the entire four days.

Thus, it's essential to understand factors that affect individuals and how individuals go about making purchasing decisions. It's only then that companies can get the right products to the right people and effectively market and sell goods and services. Once companies understand consumers, they can use strategies to mine this knowledge and use it to ensure their products and services are marketed to the right individuals at the right time.

By understanding the consumer buying process, purchase involvement and the various internal and external factors that affect consumer behaviour, entrepreneurs can better understand their target audience and cater to them. They can take advantage of their knowledge of consumer psychology and behaviour and use this to increase sales and effectively grow their businesses. Thus, understanding consumer behaviour and why they buy is the key to ensuring consumers buy from you instead of from your competition.

NAILA QAZI

Being raised in Chiniot, a small, rural town in Pakistan, was undoubtedly an ideal space to pick up an entrepreneurial spirit. I was always a curious child. I enjoyed going to the market with my granddad, who was a local farmer. I observed the buying and selling environment at an early age. I picked the right values to build a business, which manifested in my life's later stages.

I have travelled around the world and have lived and worked on several continents. I ran several businesses successfully and worked in diverse sectors, including transportation, consultation, education, technology and business. With success, I also confronted failures, especially when it came to the consumers. The consumer mindset is the critical and deciding factor for a business. Through different entrepreneurial endeavours, I learned deeply about consumer behaviour and its implications for the success of a business.

LEVERAGING INTELLECTUAL PROPERTY RIGHTS

Pooja Bhatia

Introduction

Intellectual Property Rights (IPRs) are a cardinal class of assets for an organisation. Any organisation, including a startup, can derive benefits by effectively leveraging it. This is only possible when Intellectual Property (IP) is protected and protected efficiently. Unprotected IP generally passes into public domain and loses its enforceability. The other factors influencing enforceability of IPR depend upon jurisdiction, whether the scope is limited, the ownership is clear and if it is maintained in any of the jurisdictions where it is protected. In order to have good brand value, startups need to ensure that they are not infringing on anyone else's right and also avoid the legal burden. Unfortunately, in most organisations, the IPR is lost before it is captured because of lack of awareness, policy framework flaws and hazards of financial implications. It is essential to involve a mentor in the early stages to guide on various IPR matters, rather than engaging at a later stage when it may be too late.

Venturing into intellectual property

Up to 2006, I was not aware of the meaning of IP and its significance, nor how integral a part of our lives it is. I was working towards getting myself registered for a PhD program in 2006 when I came across a local Indian newspaper advertisement from the Department of Science and Technology, Government of India, related to a yearlong Women Scholarship Scheme (now called 'Kiran Scheme').

The scheme intended to train women in IP and IPRs by placing them with law firms and IP cells (of various organisations). It was a competitive process; I sat for the written examination and cleared the interview. I was placed with the Intellectual Property Management Division (now the Innovation Protection Unit) of the Council for Scientific and Industrial Research.

During the training program, I learned that IP is the creation of one's mind and it becomes an IPR when the application for its protection, submitted to the respective office in a particular country, is granted. Indeed, it is jurisdictional and only enforceable where one protects it *[Box1]*. The enforceability is also subject to whether it is protected or granted, continuing validity and scope of the protection. If one has only applied for an IP, the right to enforce it does not accrue until it is granted. Similarly, IP needs to be maintained for its life term.

If IPR lapses or is abandoned, then it is no longer active/valid nor enforceable. Especially in the case of patents, one can only enforce it if the invention is captured or adequately captured in the claims portion of a patent specification. Thus, enforceability is dependent upon numerous factors that one should be cognisant of.

Box 1: Characteristics of IP

IP is:
- Local, not global.
- Enforceable where and if protected.
- An asset.
- An investment.

Different forms of intellectual property

IPRs are of diverse forms and include patents, copyright, designs, trademarks and geographical indications *[Figure 1]*. In addition, in some countries protection for plant variety, layout designs of integrated circuits and trade secrets are also counted under IPR. From a startup's point of view, the four most relevant forms of IPR are patents, trademarks, copyright and designs. It is worthy to note that trade secrets are equally important but may not be protectable in several countries under a particular statutory act. However, it may be enforceable under torts and contract law.

Figure 1: Various forms of IP and their examples

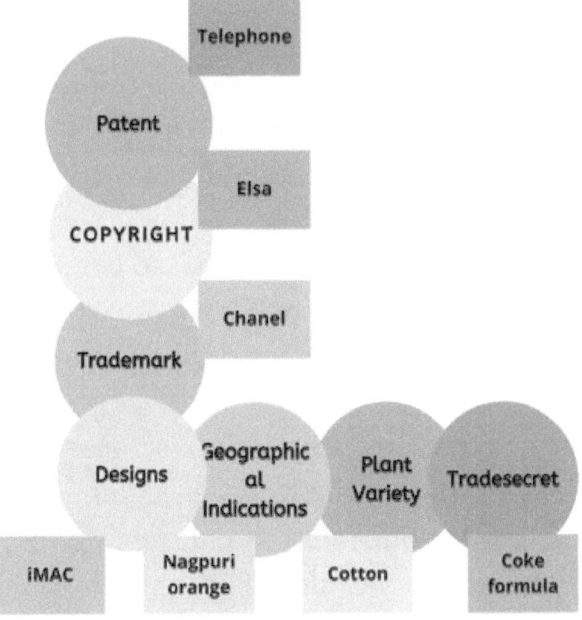

Each of the four above-described forms of IPR differ in terms of the criteria for protection, subject matter for protection, term and the application process *[Box 2]*.

Box 2: Four important tools for a startup

Patents: • Protects technology. • Twenty-year term. • Criteria: novelty, inventive step and industrial application.	Copyright: • Protects a form of expression. • Age of author + 50-95 years. • Needs to be original.
Trademark: • Protects logos, slogans, taglines, smells, trade/service names. • Ten years and renewable. • Distinct.	Designs: • Protects look and feel of a product. • Ten years + five years. • Novel.

Patents only protect the technology – be it a product or a process or both. For a patent application, besides the exclusions provided in the national laws of a country, it has to meet the three standard criteria – namely novelty, inventive step and industrial application. Patents have a term of twenty years from the date of application filing.

Trademarks protect business names, logos, slogans, smells (like a rose-scented tyre), sound (lion roar of MGM) and shapes (a classic example of Coca-Cola bottles). Trademarks are renewable every ten years, provided the mark is still in use. While design only protects the aesthetic look and needs to be original and have novelty, which means it is not published or displayed anywhere before applying. Designs are granted for ten years and renewed for another five years.

Copyright covers a spectrum of subject matter from literal, musical, dramatic and artistic work, including software to performers and broadcasting rights. It only lends protection to the way of expression but not to ideas, facts or methods of operation.

However, the way the content is expressed and arranged in manuals, databases and websites is protectable under copyright. Another interesting fact about copyright is that it accrues the moment the content is created. However, it needs to be registered for its enforceability. It is also the one of the IPRs with the longest validity. For a literary work, the term is the age of the author plus from fifty to ninety-five years (depending upon the country).

The application process is different and specific to the type of IPR intended to be protected and varies from country to country. However, there are four common steps involved starting from submitting the application, which is then published and later examined, and after examination, if everything is in order, it is granted or registered.

Figure 2: Career time line

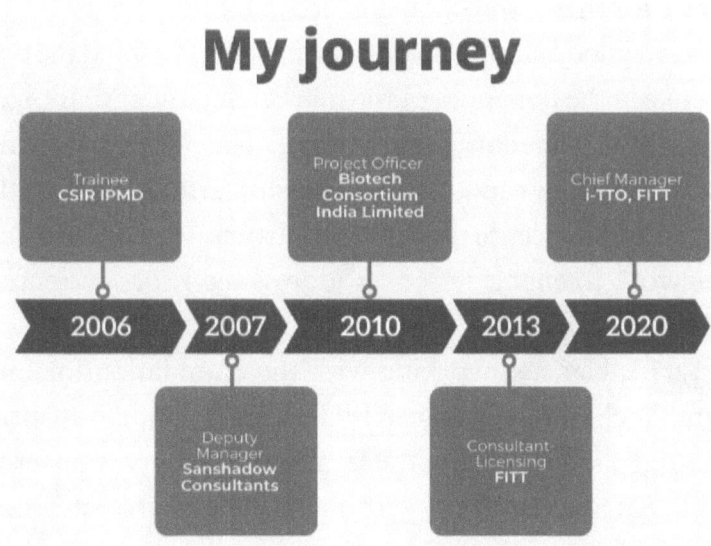

Life after the internship

Thus, one can figure out how IP started to intrigue me, and as a result, I decided to stay in this field. After completing the yearlong training program, I joined a boutique consultancy firm,

Sanshadow Consultants, with whom I worked for about two and a half years. I assisted startups and academic institutions in conducting searches to ensure that they are not reinventing the wheel, filing their IP applications and completing the requisite formalities. I also had the opportunity to work on framing IP policies for two institutions, enabling them to effectively protect and commercialise their IP.

Later, I joined Biotech Consortium India Limited, as part of the team responsible for managing IPs for the Stanford India Biodesign program. It was a collaborative program run with All India Institute of Medical Sciences and Indian Institute of Technology Delhi as partners from India and Stanford University from the United States, supported by the Department of Biotechnology, Government of India. Here I got to work on medical device inventions, devising strategies for their protection and commercialisation.

It was a good learning process for me to understand the connection between the dynamics of the market and the invention developed and how to identify the user needs. The program provided an option to the fellows and interns to create startups based on the IPs generated and to licence these to the startups. However, it required a framework to enable it and to address the issues entrepreneurs face while transferring technologies to startups.

In 2013, I started working with the Foundation for Innovation and Technology Transfer (FITT), at the Indian Institute of Technology Delhi, heading the IP and technology transfer team. The role entailed working with faculty members, students and startups facilitating IP management and technology transfer. Out of the sixty-five technologies and IP that I had transferred in the sixteen years, most were given to startups or startups were created on it, in some cases by the inventors themselves or by a third party. In some situations, the task did not end by transferring or licensing the technology or IP, it also entailed finding collaborators to work further on the development part, or manufacturers for manufacturing or finding funding resources.

It was both challenging and exciting to crack a technology transfer deal. I also had a sense of satisfaction as I was helping to bring technologies for the benefit of society. Being in the field of licensing and technology transfer, I was keen to have a certification endorsing my expertise. While interacting with peer tech transfer professionals in technology transfer offices in the States and Europe, I observed most had Certified Licensing Professional (CLP) and Registered Technology Transfer Professional (RTTP) designations.

I decided to pursue these certifications and earned one after another in 2018 and 2019, and become the fourth in India to have CLP designation and the first RTTP.

2020 & beyond

Moving forward, the year 2020 brought two opportunities along with it. One was to be a mother to a wonderful baby girl, and the second was to set up and lead Innovation-Technology Transfer Office (i-TTO) at FITT.

National Biopharma Mission, a joint project of the World Bank and Department of Biotechnology, Government of India, implemented by the Biotechnology Industry Research Assistance Council, set out to create and support seven technology transfer offices.

i-TTO was one of the seven technology transfer offices, set up at FITT. Not only did I design the logo for i-TTO but also curated different offerings for the stakeholders. I worked with startups, entrepreneurs, innovators and academic institutions. New models to provide the necessary support to the stakeholders were crafted.

Despite the COVID-19 pandemic, numerous initiatives to promote and support entrepreneurship were undertaken.

My assigned role was to ensure that i-TTO is up and running and becomes self-sustained and striving. It was also critical for me to bring in a change in the ecosystem. More than two hundred webinars, on different aspects of entrepreneurship, IP and technology transfer, were conducted.

Managing two babies at the same time was a daunting job, but I thoroughly enjoyed it. Both helped in making a better version of myself. I learned different perspectives and became more creative. As my daughter grew, curiosity was at its best, and mobility fastest, thereby, necessity was the mother of invention, so I kept innovating ways to manage things. I used the twenty-minute rule for both professional and household chores. I would keep my daughter engaged with different games and use those twenty minutes to complete a task. But it required planning and breaking up tasks into small steps.

The plans would change or modify based on the urgencies and emergencies. Alongside, I developed a principle to applaud myself for whatever could be achieved, in any case, if not the least I had my daughter smiling. I created a support network for myself, talking to not only my friends and family but also with other fellow mothers exchanging notes and tricks. I adapted my routine accordingly to my daughter's needs. Before I share about the next stage of my life, I want to illustrate how startups can leverage IP.

Abundance of myths & misconceptions

During the sessions, as we interacted with the startups and academia, it was understood what myths and misconceptions around IP exist *[Box 3]*.

It was heartening to see how both startups and academic institutions were changing their perspective and placing importance on IP. Most organisations, though, waited for the right time to file applications and sometimes missed the bus.

Box 3: General myths revolving around IP

> Demystifying myths:
> - No term as global IP.
> - File IP earlier rather than later.
> - You can file it on your own, however, you need to be careful of the laws and practices.
> - Don't save cost at the cost of your work.

Some would be focusing on just one form of IP and ignoring others, however, they would have gained more if they had a variety of eggs in the basket. Having different forms of IP is also beneficial to use as a branding and marketing tool. Though trademarks and designs are most commonly used for branding, copyright too can play a role. A portfolio of IP serves as an entry barrier for others as one is creating a monopoly in that particular market. It could also be instrumental to raise investment through government grants and private funding.

In most startups, the relevant framework is missing, which can assist in addressing issues of ownership. In one instance, one of the startups had engaged a technical advisor working with a university. They planned to file the patent application with the technical advisor named as one of the inventors.

Few clarifications were sought before initiating the patent application. It was checked with them if they had an agreement with the technical advisor if they can specify his contribution in terms of the conception of the idea and reducing it to practice. In addition, if there were any terms and conditions of the university. To my surprise, the startup thought these were unnecessary questions; later, it was explained to them why these were critical from a patent law perspective.

Similarly, in another case, the startup was filing all its IP in the founders' names instead of the startup itself, missing the opportunity to create an asset for the company. Thus, a policy can help in defining the ownership. It can also cover the mechanism to decide inventor/authorship and revenue sharing, the process to be followed by an employee or an intern, authorities for signing, etc.

It is also essential to not just have the framework in place, but it needs to percolate to all levels, so that all should be aware of the policy. In another scenario, the company engaged consultants and vendors for a certain part of the project and ended up losing their IP as the agreements executed stated the IP would be shared, though the vendors/consultants had not contributed to either conception or reduction.

Many were unaware that there is no such thing as global IP as you have to protect IP in every country where you wish to enter or market your products or services. Another common mistake is looking for low cost or doing it yourself to save money, but is it worth it to ensure that you are getting the best service. To decide that, check the credentials the person or the company has, the work done so far, get test work done or seek advice on an issue. The quality and strength of the IP will have a direct impact when one is trying to sell or license it.

What is technology transfer & how to leverage it

Technology transfer or IP licensing can be a critical tool for startups and entrepreneurs. Technology transfer is the process of transferring technology, data, IP, materials (prototype, biological materials) and know-how (or trade secrets) from one organisation to another or an individual to an organisation.

There are three modes of transferring technology, namely know-how transfer (non-IP protected), assigned (protected IP) or licensed (IP protected). Upon transfer of unprotected technology, it will no longer remain a trade secret unless the other organisation takes care of it. In the case of assignment or acquisition too, the entire rights are acquired, therefore, the originator cannot use it any further, while upon licensing, one can retain the ownership, giving others the right to use, sell or make.

Licensing is of two main types: non-exclusive, where IPR is licensed to multiple companies, or exclusive, which means IPR is licensed to a single company. Both have their advantages and disadvantages. When a startup is licensing-in, exclusivity would be a good option, and while licensing-out, both types could be used depending upon the IP to be licensed.

Instead of creating everything from scratch, one can take a licence or acquire the IPRs already there. This will help in investing at the right place, with IP already protected, and getting a collaborator to work on its further development. One needs to scout for the right fit, which will depend upon a lot of factors, but essentially one needs to know where to look. Academic institutions are a common source for IP licensing, they also help entrepreneurs to create startups based on their IP.

In the academic setting, however, IP is never transferred to an individual, it has to be an entity. Most organisations, other than academic institutions, frequently have some portfolio of their IP that they are looking to monetise. Once the relevant technology or IP is identified, financials come into the picture and negotiation begins. As a culmination, an agreement is executed, giving the startup the right to do certain things.

The entire process could be quick or may take some months to close. Besides taking in an IP or technology from another organisation, one can opt to transfer or licence the IP or technology to another organisation, if there is a portfolio of IP or an IP or technology that is no longer required. Therefore saving costs, avoiding killing something that one has created and generating a new source of revenue. When one licences it to another organisation, a signing amount, milestone payments, royalties or maybe even equity would also be negotiated, generating funding for more innovations.

Birth of 'Inoberry'

After my two-year stint as a chief manager, I took a break to be a hands-on mom. Many startups, entrepreneurs and innovators connected with me during my break. Some continued to reach out to me to assist them with IP and technology transfer matters. This prompted me to concentrate on devising ways to club my expertise in helping startups and entrepreneurs while enjoying motherhood.

Box 4: Characteristics of a strong trademark

A trademark should be:
- Distinctive.
- Short.
- Easy to pronounce and spell.
- Descriptive of services or products intended to offer.

Therefore, I decided to become a founder, and Inoberry was born. A three-step process to create 'Inoberry' as the company name was adopted. I first decided upon what services and products I would be offering. Based on the offerings, by combinations and permutations, ten unique names were generated. I also decided to have sub-brands for each service and product, with Inoberry as the main company. I ensured that the names I was framing were coined words, which means these words do not exist in the dictionary, do not have a secondary meaning in any language, nor are related to or convey the services or products of the company, aka should not be descriptive.

Generally, descriptive marks are a weak form of trademark, while coined words are the strongest. Last but not least, it should be catchy and appealing. Then I started with another three steps; I checked for the domain name from two to three websites and shortlisted two that were available. The next step was to check whether these or similar trademarks were already filed, whether live or dead, using the trademark database of various countries like India and the United States and the World Intellectual Property Office Global Brand Database. And lastly, I cross-checked if the company name was available for registration, or if it was already taken.

Through these three steps, I wanted to ensure that I was not infringing on anyone else's IP, but rather creating a non-infringing asset for my company. This was just for the name – I repeated most of the same processes for the logo and the taglines. The process did not end at this step, I have gone further and created a user guide to ensure that the names, logos and taglines are used as per the specified dimensions and colours and in the correct way to keep their value intact. The more one respects one's IP, the more valuable it will become.

The importance of IP

'A stitch in time saves nine' is applicable in all walks of life, but in particular, it is aptly applicable for IPR. A right step in the right direction, at the right time, saves from pain later on, thus, knowing what IP is and how to leverage it is essential. This chapter will help one understand the key aspects of IP management and serve as a motivation to build an IP portfolio. Nevertheless, one would need to frame strategies to effectively protect the IP. However, one needs to remember that every situation is different, and copy-and-pasting a strategy that worked for others may not work in the current situation. No strategy is one fits all; it is as unique as is the IP.

So, my key takeaways are simple but impactful:
- Framing relevant organisational policies and framework is critical to enable capturing IP, define ownership and effective management of the overall process.
- Guides for proper usage of the trademarks.
- Thorough examination of agreements for any IP-related implications.
- It is better to be safe. Thus, conduct searches diligently to avoid reinventing the wheel and to cross-check for probable infringement.

POOJA BHATIA

I help innovators and organisations transform their ideas to innovations, preventing them from reinventing the wheel and transferring technologies. I hold an MBA degree in technology management, two internally recognised credentials – certified licensing professional, registered technology transfer professional – and am a registered patent agent with the Indian Patent Office.

I was earlier heading Innovation-Technology Transfer Office (i-TTO) of the Foundation for Innovation and Technology Transfer (FITT) in New Delhi, India, as the chief manager. I have worked with academia, startups and incubation centres for innovation management and technology transfer. My work entails innovation management, technology transfer, marketing, strategic partnership, industry engagement and policy development. I serve on various committees including the CLP Exam Development and Maintenance committee.

I have over sixteen years of professional experience in intellectual property, licensing, collaborations and policy framing, and am a recipient of Global Women Leader Award 2021, Best Woman Mentor Award – International Inspirational Women Awards 2021, runner-up to Women Power Impact Creator 2021 and WIPF Powerful Women In IP 2021.

My motto is to simplify legal aspects of innovation management and technology transfer. Thereby, reducing the gap and increasing the number of products from lab to bedside. Framing strategies for effective management and negotiation are my strong points. I believe in empathy, and I like to read books and cook.

FIND YOUR OWN WAY

Sarah Blake

Who remembers being asked, 'What do you want to be when you grow up?' If you were anything like me, I struggled to put words to what I wanted to do. I knew deep down that I wanted to make a difference – a big difference, think global difference – but I just didn't know what that was. I grew up in a small country town, where thinking big went as far as the next district, but even then, you'd be expected to come home. This unspoken pressure was especially true for women, and I never fit that mould. My brothers got sent to boarding school to expand their opportunities, but without this chance myself, I learnt early on that if I was to make a difference it was up to me to drive it.

Fast-forward through the early years of university, life, self-discovery and a plan started to form. Not a clear plan, just a sense of purpose and that I was heading where I needed to. When I reflect on the genesis of my desire for business domination, I think it started from my deep sense of self and my inner core which has always believed in 'me'. This grounding has always been there – through the hard times of life and the celebrations – and has given me the confidence to reach high.

This grounding has led me to where I am now, a multi-award-winning conflict strategist and mediator. I have grown a successful company and this growth keeps expanding. I am a bestselling author and regularly contribute to the media on all things conflict. But the things I am most proud of are the quiet moments of empowering others to navigate hard conversations and conflict with grace and wisdom. See, I am unapologetic about both success and my desire to make a difference. We need to walk the talk.

Too often in media, books and throughout the business world, we see examples of success that celebrate the masculine, uncompromising financial interpretation of success, but as women, this picture doesn't always align. The barriers that we face as female entrepreneurs make it even harder, with data from Crunchbase indicating that only about 2.3% of venture capital goes to women.[1] The fact that business 'success' is judged on a gender bias lens means that these notions of success will often feel uncomfortable for women.

In my experience, these traditional notions of success feel inauthentic, they just don't sit right. What I see from many women is that it places more pressure on them to conform to a normalised notion of business success. Work harder, longer and be more ruthless. Keep going until you reach for some unattainable perfection. But isn't there enough pressure on us already to do everything and be everything for everyone else? What I want you to consider in reading this chapter is that BUSINESS DOMINATION is what you define for yourself. Yes, it is about financial, professional and even personal success, but that success will look very different for everyone.

1) forbes.com/sites/forbesbusinesscouncil/2021/09/21/overcoming-some-of-the-barriers-to-women-entrepreneurship/?sh=2342f89e2780 article published on 21 September 2021, accessed on 28 August 2022.

I want this chapter to be practical and useful to you, something that isn't just theory but provides steps that you can do. As professional women we have so much knowledge, what we often need is examples of inspiration to make it real. I hope sharing my insights into what has guided me along my business domination journey will plant some seeds for your own success.

Personal development

So, before you jump up and shout that you do development all the time, just hold a moment and let me explain. Personal development is distinct from professional development. Personal development is having the courage to look inside at both your strengths and your weaknesses, of reflecting and making a commitment to you as a whole person not just as a professional.

It is actually hard work, it requires discipline and action, but once that door is open it is an incredibly rewarding lifelong journey. My journey has not always been rosy, certainly there have been times where I felt despair deep in my soul, but I have always used this to catapult my adventure to the next level of insight, knowing and doing.

This personal journey also requires that you put your ego on hold – perhaps not just on hold but on notice. Personal development is about examining our ego – warts, diamonds and all. There is a vulnerability in it, so it feels uncomfortable and sometimes painful. Which seems contradictory to the 'perfect image' and PR messages that flood us on what success means. Personal development, the type that is a gritty, honest and grounded reflection, is what enables us to walk authentically and empowers us to connect deeply with those around us. This gritty ego helps keep the heart and head aligned and balanced so that we can soar in a way that is sustainable without compromising our values.

But why does this matter? As you transition from a business to business domination you are investing in not just your technical expertise but your personal capacity. Often it is your own bias, barriers and baggage that is stopping you from growing and if we can't take responsibility for that, then we will never reach that next level.

My own personal development journey has been a dance to my own adventure. Sometimes fast and deep, and sometimes a slow trickle. Certainly, there have been times where I felt lost, where I failed and made mistakes, but these moments too have provided the biggest lessons for growth.

I am incredibly grateful for the foundations provided by my parents, who in their own ways encouraged self-reflection and a curious, learning mindset. Growing up, we had a strong focus on reflection, listening and ritual – this was a spirituality that embraced nature, learning and generosity. I was also blessed by my maternal family whose connections to country, to community and to the practical realities of life, taught me to balance the head and heart – to walk the talk, as they say.

This grounding has informed my professional practice and my personal life. It has meant that I always ask myself, *What have I contributed to and what can I learn from this?* But this personal development journey hasn't always been easy, in fact, my biggest learnings without a doubt have always emerged from the most painful times in my life. And for that reason, I never regret or wish that things had been different.

There are events that stand out in terms of having deeply shaped who I am today and the confidence I bring to my work. In hindsight, these are the moments that I consciously decided to lean into deep personal reflection and was brave enough to feel the pain. My personal development journey is not one moment but rather a gathering of experiences. From retreats, mentors, professional supervision and a small inner circle – what has been consistent is the time out to self-reflect on where I am, how I am and what I want to change moving forward.

There is a standout though, my participation in the Mawul Rom: Cross Cultural Mediation and Leadership course. Every year for nearly ten years, I was lucky enough to be a participant and contribute to this immersive project that gathered Indigenous and non-Indigenous people from across the country to come together to learn what mutual respect really means.

This experience changed me. It forced me to examine my own assumptions, bias and privilege. It provided space for deep reflection and connection on an annual basis. The ritual of the learning spaces grounded me and uplifted my spirit. I learnt from this about my history genealogically, my history as a nation and my place in the world. I learnt about my values and the importance of aligning action with words authentically. I learnt about caring for myself and valuing my own personal development as a distinct aspect of professional growth. It helped me gain clarity about the things that were core to me. These are some of the things I know are true for me:

- Respect for spirit. Whilst the naming may change for each of us – be it spiritual, religious or other – my personal development is grounded in the connection to and trust in life. My belief, my spirituality and my optimism allows room for the magic of life to unfold. This does not absolve me of responsibility, rather it becomes a privileged responsibility to align authentically my actions.
- Valuing of self. I remember in year twelve someone saying to me that I always seem so confident, what I said then remains true,

'I am blessed – whether by nature or nurture – to have a deep sense of purpose, value and belief in me.' This hasn't always made life easy – people often interpreted that as arrogance when I was young. But it is also a gift; I am proud of me, I have never suffered imposter syndrome because when it comes down to it, I really am proud of and like me. But it is also something to nurture, to reconnect with and to reflect on – where am I at, am I prioritising me and what can I do to uplift my soul.

- Commitment to peace-making, not conflict-denying. The work of personal development has meant that I am also driven by a desire to serve, give back and contribute to positive change rather than self-gratification. I have always felt like I was put here with a purpose, but the personal development work helped me connect to what it is. When there is clarity of purpose, it becomes much easier to put aside ego. The reality check, *Is what I am doing aligned to or contributing to making a difference or is my ego getting in the way?*

A personal development journey isn't an easy path – to do it with integrity requires honest reflection, a reality check, and sometimes we need help with that. Our egos stop us seeing things others might. So here are my top tips to help you on your own journey:

1. Always make time to just be. Schedule time for reflection, writing and calm, away from the pressure to deliver, because if you can't create those reflective moments, you will burnout, you will stagnate.
2. Every year dedicate a few days to focus on your business away from everyone – this is just you looking forward. This will help you create clarity of focus and vision.

3. Find a mentor or supervisor – not just professionally but personally, you need someone who will challenge you gently and hold you when you stumble.

These lessons and more remain critical to who I am today. They form part of my ongoing personal development dance. A reflection, a nurturing and a joy.

Business advice

Honestly, this notion of 'business advice' is so subjective. On your business journey you will hear so much 'good advice', 'well-meaning' insights and downright sabotaging rubbish. So rather than try and convince you of the answer, I want to challenge you to think about good processes, because if you follow a good process, you will reach the decisions that are right for you at the right time.

What you do, what is right for you, is so unique to your own story so before you go and seek experts really understand what matters to you and why.

Along my entrepreneurial journey, I have always been alert to and conscious of the need for good advice. I'm not sure if this is my background in anthropology, always questioning assumptions, or my role as a mediator, which allows me to recognise that rarely does one person have all the answers. Whatever the reason, I love to learn and have always been open to advice. But there is tension. I am also conscious that there have been occasions when I have let doubt stop me trusting my instincts and my knowledge base. I was looking for validation or an expert to make it all okay, when the reality is that whilst I need the best advice from experts, I also have to temper that with internal trust. What lets me navigate this is … a good process.

So, instead of advice, there are questions that you need to wrestle with. These questions will help you develop a good process of reflection, research, action – the praxis.

Business question one
Am I taking my business seriously and what measures indicate this?
The level of your commitment impacts how you move forward.
Many women, whether in service or sales, allow the intimidation of structure, financial planning and professional and legal needs intimidate them. If you are serious about your business, you need to take all aspects of it seriously, not just the doing.

The pivot point for me in shifting from just a business to domination was the mental shift of really taking the business seriously, not just the profession. When this shift happens, your thinking necessarily becomes more strategic. You recognise your limitations as well as your strengths.

Tip: skills gap mapping
Make the time to map out not just your professional expertise but your business strengths and weaknesses. This will help you identify your skills, knowledge, and technical gaps. Once you have this you can prioritise based on your own needs. Consider how you might fill those gaps – is it something that you need to know or something that someone else can help you with?

Don't beat yourself up if you get it wrong either. We all have lessons to learn. In the early stages of transition with my business I knew I needed a mentor, I did my research, I spoke with friends and reference checked. I found someone – and whilst they were good for a period of about six months – flags started to appear. Instead of listening to these I let self-doubt cloud my decision and stayed much too long. It ended up costing me way too much money with very little tangible return. Lesson learnt – trust my instincts and be really specific when engaging a consultant.

Business question two
Have you codified your decision-making processes?

We're business professionals so we are great at decision-making, right?! Bursting your bubble is not something I enjoy, but the reality is that whilst you may have moments of greatness, unless you have brought discipline and structure to your decision-making process, it is likely the good luck will be unsustainable.

I'm all about good process, but it is perhaps an undervalued skill in this era of instant gratification and fast ego expertise. Creating a clear and consistent decision-making process will be critical as you grow and the levels of complexity increase. There are different types of decisions you will be making – fast, everyday decisions and big, strategic decisions.[2] The art is in identifying the difference and holding back to create space not reaction.

Good process, the discipline of honouring it, will help you critically analyse the 'advice you get' and temper the instinct to respond. What you want to achieve is a balance between your emotive instinctual response and rational thinking brain. Having your process up on your wall to remind you will help you to pause before you commit.

Tip: decision-making process design
Whatever model you use, the structure and discipline of the process will help you reduce the risk of things going wrong or of making poor choices. As you become more familiar with your process, it will become quicker and more instinctual. For me, I often have

---
2) D Kahneman, *Thinking Fast and Slow,* Published 2011, Penguin Books.

a rapid turnaround for decisions, because they have become systemised. But I also make sure that in big decisions I pause.

A simple decision-making process may look like:

- Name: Recognise and name the problem, conflict or gap to be addressed.
- Explore: Research and critically analyse with curiosity not a fixed mindset.
- Challenge: Consider options, alternatives and realities.
- Hold: Pause to ensure rationale and emotions are aligned.
- Engage: Commit to your decision and implement.

As you grow it will likely be helpful to distinguish the BIG issues from the EVERYDAY issues. What are the topics that require disciplined decision-making and what issues are you happy to allow to flow fast.

Business question three
Have you identified your knowledge, skills and technical gaps?

You may feel superhuman, or perhaps you are still swept up in the notion that your idea will change the world. Look, that is fantastic, that joy and enthusiasm will get you through the hard times – but you are also human and not a supercomputer. There are things you don't know, things you won't be great at and somewhere along the line you will fail or make mistakes. Don't let this crush you. The trick is to have a plan, and understanding the risks is where we start.

The reality is that as you level up you need to become better at identifying and recognising the risks – like you can't do it all, all the time. This is why finding the right business support is so important; but rather than just throwing your hand up and taking advice from every 'Joe blow', you need to become strategic, focused and discerning.

There is a vulnerability in this, of recognising that you don't know it all. And if you find it hard, know that many high-performing people also find it difficult to ask for help. People worry that others might think less of them, there is shame and fear. Brené Brown[3] talks about this barrier, acknowledging that it takes 'real courage to be vulnerable', and if you don't ask, you create barriers to growth. In the early days of your business journey, the reality is that money is often tight, so you try and do everything yourself. This is okay for a short time, but it doesn't help you level up sustainably. Instead, it limits your growth because you create information barriers, you don't address those gaps and you make decisions based on poor information.

I know this is hard to do – trust me, I can be a bit of a perfectionist, I want everything right before I ask for help. It isn't so much about being embarrassed or not knowing, for me it has been this self-judgement that somehow, I should know. I quickly got over this – recognising the limiting belief that it was. Now, instead, I take the time to really consider what those knowledge and skill gaps are, I weigh the value of me learning and doing versus the value of someone else doing. If investment is needed, I plan out what I can afford now and what plan I can put in place to earn the funds to do what I need. Now I dedicate my time to where I can really contribute to change and seek advice and expertise for the areas that I can't.

Honestly, great leaders are the people who embrace these gaps and address them – they don't try to bluff their way through, pretend to be experts at everything. Great leaders create collaborative

---
3) B Brown, 2018, *Dare to Lead: Brave Work. Tough Conversations. Whole Hearts,* London, Vermilion.

teams and partnerships with people who share values, *whys* or vision – and they nurture the respective strengths.

So, find the people that can fill the gaps, share the load or bring the specialist skills to your growth plan. But don't hand over your power – you must remain empowered throughout the process of levelling up. This is distinct from micromanaging everything and is instead keeping your hand on the pulse, asking lots of questions and creating accountability both for you and your experts.

Tip: conduct six-to-twelve-monthly gap analysis
This again is about developing good process habits, so make the time to regularly review your skills, knowledge and technical gaps. What are you doing well, where might you improve, what do you feel confident about and what perhaps is causing you some stress? Remember – stress is a critical indicator that there is something here that needs to be addressed.

With the analysis done, it is time to take action. Find the right fit but don't just go for the shiny bells and whistle, ask questions, listen to your instincts and validate insights with critical evidence and research.

These process-focused tips will, I hope, help you navigate the minefield of people offering you well-meaning business advice. Honestly, what I have learnt and what guides me best is remembering that every interaction is an opportunity to learn. I am open to listening, I am curious about ideas and I have a deep trust in my own ability to navigate this space.

Overcoming adversity

If reading about the challenges of business domination isn't daunting enough and if you thought the list of skills you needed was huge, then brace yourself, there is more! One of the defining secrets of business domination is our ability to navigate and overcome adversity.

The statistics around new businesses that fail are huge, with only 78.5% of small businesses surviving the first year[4] and Forbes suggest that 90%[5] startups fail. This means that the success rate of entrepreneurs who hit the BIG time is small. But that doesn't seem to stop us trying; call us optimistic, passionately driven or just plain stubborn, for those of us trying to increase our economic opportunities and make a difference in the world, becoming an entrepreneur is the 'hot career move'. But it isn't all smooth sailing – well to be honest, those moments of calm are usually few and far between!

As a conflict strategist, my whole career has been about walking in this grey space of conflict, uncertainty and adversity. I have watched the mistakes and I have witnessed the costs. For me, I can't walk the talk of dispute resolution if I lack integrity – so my mindset resets every time I am faced with adversity – this is not a setback but rather an opportunity.

So, to keep it real I thought I would share some of the adversities that I have wrestled with and what I have learnt.

Adversity challenge one: balancing parenthood and work

As a mum of two young boys and with a husband in the forces, I have had to learn to be adaptive, resilient and flexible. Those of you with lots of competing demands likely know the feeling. It is hard work – so how do I handle the ongoing adversity of juggling life? There is no magic wand, but I have gotten better at being present.

---

4) fortunly.com/statistics/small-business-failure-statistics/#gref published 18 January 2022, accessed 28 August 2022.
5) forbes.com/sites/neilpatel/2015/01/16/90-of-startups-will-fail-heres-what-you-need-to-know-about-the-10/?sh=f8fd97966792 January 2015, accessed August 2022.

Whether it is sick kids, school holidays or just the juggle of running life, you stay grounded by checking in your prioritisation. I allocate time for work and time for my family. I have learnt (well, continue to learn) to be gentle with myself. That sometimes you have to let go of a plan and adapt to the new one. It will be okay – everyone else is dealing with the same stuff, we just don't talk about it. So don't be apologetic about prioritising kids and family – success doesn't have to mean work before family.

Adversity challenge two: when an idea fails
Somewhere along the line it's likely that you will fail. An idea will flop, you will make a mistake, or you might even make someone angry and create conflict. This is normal, and if you manage it well you just might grow from the experience. I have done all these things, but with each moment I have paused to reflect on what I might have done differently and what I can take forward into the future.

My first foray into running a company was with a colleague, and within twelve months we realised that the partnership wasn't going to work. We both had different expectations about what it meant to own a company. So, whilst that company folded, I don't regret it. The process gave me the confidence to step out on my own, I learnt about what to do and what to avoid, and I improved. I took what was disappointing and turned it around into something I am so proud of.

Adversity challenge three: COVID-19 pressure
The world paused; business staggered, and people died. The realities of the impact of COVID-19 are still being identified and understood but it has certainly caused significant stress for many in the business and entrepreneurial space. We each

had decisions to make and choices to weigh. Many became overwhelmed, some lost their income streams and others just couldn't continue. But it has also been a time of innovation, growth and opportunity.

Like many, COVID-19 impacted our family and has significantly impacted my industry. But rather than let it overwhelm me, I recognised and named my fears and problems, I felt it and then I let it inform how I moved forward. I recognise my limitations and just did what was possible, it has slowed down growth but also enabled me to refocus my energy. It gave me the space to really clarify where I am going and how I am going to get there.

What you are probably starting to see is that your ability to overcome adversity isn't a check-box list but rather a mindset. How you interpret the problems and challenges impacts your responses. If you see them as a threat, something to be fearful of, you are more likely to have a high stress response and high emotions get in the way of effective problem solving.

Tip: adjust your mindset

As you strive for business domination you also need to adjust your mindset. You need to develop a leadership style that sees confusion, conflict and difference not as a bad thing but as an opportunity. These experiences are there for us to learn from – you may not always get that perfect storybook ending, but I have no hesitation in saying that if you approach your adversities with a curious and open mind you are going to find solutions that you never expected. This isn't about 'tree hugging fluff', but it is about balancing hope with realities. In looking forward instead of looking to blame, you are more likely to find that innovation gap that will carry you toward that next level of growth.

I feel so fortunate to be doing what I am – creating financial success and making a difference. I am proud too that I haven't let anyone else define me and diminish me. In the dispute resolution world, there is a 'normal path progression'. Success is defined by being a white male of an era who has a successful legal career. There is an expectation that you follow the unspoken rules of doing the job, being quiet and grateful for what you get. None of that has ever appealed to me. I am loud when I need to be, creative in how I meet the needs of the market and proud that I am finding my own way.

Business domination isn't a destination but rather an aspiration to make a difference both to my family and the community more widely. Success is what I define it as, the measure I use works for me and any accolade is a bonus.

Sarah's five tips to business domination as a woman

1. Create a mindset aligned to your values and your vision
Your mindset shapes not just your future but how others respond to you. If it isn't aligned to your values, your success lacks authenticity. You need to discover this for yourself, you need to invest in your mindset and then ground it into your soul. This will give you the confidence to navigate the traps, challenges and negativity that emerges throughout the process of growth.

2. Don't be apologetic about wanting to be successful
Too often, women in particular underplay and diminish their desire for success. Levelling up requires that you own this, own your own power. Success will look different for each of you – that is the wonderful thing about this journey. But as entrepreneurs you are striving to creating multiple incomes streams that give

you the freedom to influence, change and service in the best way you can. This is amazing!

3. Create clear boundaries

Business domination is about working smarter not harder. Take the time to establish your own set of rules about what is and isn't okay – this may change, but each adjustment is considered and negotiated. In having this clarity, it will help you navigate with integrity. It will help you define your time, it will help you push back and disengage from drama and pressures that aren't yours to hold.

4. Good process creates better outcomes

Good process isn't just about helping you make good decisions, good process will help you to upscale what you do. Clarity about what, why and how will enable you to share your knowledge and bring others onboard with confidence. Yes, it takes a little more time, but the benefits mean that when you BOOM, you boom with class.

5. Collaborate with aligned women

The most successful women I know are those who have created incredible collaborations and teams. These women don't let intimidation or cattiness get in the way, they don't buy into the competitive diminishing of other women. Collaborating isn't about giving everything, nor bringing everyone in, be discerning about who you let into your inner circle. Invest the time to create a team that is diverse, values curiosity and has clarity about roles. When you know what you are working towards, when there is trust, you can weather even the harshest storm.

SARAH BLAKE

Award-winning conflict strategist and mediator, TEDx speaker and bestselling author, Sarah Blake, elevates leaders, empowering them to overcome conflict barriers. Bringing clarity to complex decision-making during confusion, conflict and crisis, she helps transform problems into opportunities.

As a second-generation mediator with over twenty-six years of experience, Sarah has engaged in some of the most complex problem situations across remote Australia and into the Pacific. She has worked within corporate, university and NFP sectors delivering intervention and is increasingly sought by leaders struggling with the impact of conflict and change.

Working across industries has provided opportunities to engage with bodies such as the World Bank, BHP, Australian Federal

Police, Land Councils and national, state and local government. Sarah has delivered talks across the world, both in person and online, and is considered a thought leader within the industry. This has enabled her to contribute to international advisory boards and support the development of the next generation of peacemakers.

She is an accredited mediator with Resolution Institute and International Mediation Institute and is the Australian Ambassador for Mediate Guru and an Ambassador for Think Network UK. Sarah is also a multiple-bestselling author and regular contributor to media in Australia including television, radio and print where she is talking all things conflict from growth leaderships, people dynamics and culture.

HOW TO MAINTAIN MOMENTUM IN BUSINESS

Shelia Farr

The ability to maintain forward momentum and excellence in your business requires you to be innovative in the way you run your business. Challenging times, such as a global pandemic, provide opportunities for business owners to reinvent themselves, but how do you continue to propel your business forward, even when times are good? To remain relevant and maintain a viable business, it is important to develop a carefully planned and well-executed approach that's fresh. Finding new ways to meet the needs of your customers and build your network to share those new strategies can help you become – or remain – a leader in business.

We have all looked for ways to reinvent ourselves in business, and collaborating with other business owners is a great way to do just that. Sharing informative presentations and using diverse panels for discussions that are interactive can revive stagnant businesses and open the door to new ways to collaborate and broaden one's sphere of influence. It can give a struggling business a great boost and can allow a thriving business to engage in new and different avenues of networking. It also helps to provide the social interaction that is so crucial to long-term job engagement and job satisfaction.

Business growth opportunities often present themselves when you know the right people, so one important thing business owners need to be focusing on – in good times and in bad times – is collaboration. Finding the right person to help share information about your business and products or services can help grow your business by leaps and bounds. This is especially true during times of economic challenge, a global pandemic, or even during periods of stagnation – when entrepreneurs are all trying to connect and help each other stay afloat. Additionally, with so many people now transitioning to remote, online and hybrid working situations, the potential to network across the world has become greater and greater. Collaborating on projects, sharing information and opportunities and connecting on a global level has now become easier than ever.

Entrepreneurship has always been a journey of challenges and perseverance. In times when a business is thriving, or even in slumps or downturns, uncertainty can arise for entrepreneurs and small business owners. However, it is precisely those times when the most opportunities for reinvention and growth present themselves. Collaboration is one way to make a huge difference and that's why I recommend focusing on being innovative and networking when considering reinvention or trying to maintain momentum in business. Once can do this not just by building new, valuable connections, but also keeping your existing contacts apprised of your goals, progress and new ways of providing goods or services. Communicating across a strong network of customers and business associates can help you not only survive but thrive.

Another way to remain successful in business is to strive to excel. Beginning a journey towards achieving personal excellence requires courage, while continuing that journey is even more difficult.

The difference between winning and struggling can easily be determined by how bold an individual is willing to be when making decisions. While some people get stuck in-between what to do and what not to do, high performers immediately take actions towards their goals.

People living with a mediocre mindset often work to find shortcuts while avoiding the amount of dedication and hard work it requires to complete the task. They never really think about taking a leap of faith. They are afraid of their own success and limit themselves in all aspects of their life. On the other hand, there are people who have the spark of excitement needed for personal excellence, but they're unable to live up to their maximum potential. Sometimes this happens in entrepreneurship, but it can also happen when you're part of a corporate team.

I will never forget the word that changed my professional life forever: acquisition.

For nearly six years, I had worked days, nights, weekends and holidays to build a dynamic team of high-producing professionals who loved what they did and achieved unbelievable results in patient care and business. We actually had a well-balanced team that loved what they did and worked hard to stay at the top of their game. That's why, the day I heard the 'A' word, my whole heart sank, and I hung my head in total defeat.

You see, when you're working to build someone else's dream, you put the key to your happiness in someone else's pocket. You give them complete control of your livelihood and your ability to impact others and the work they do. When you work for other people, it's true you don't have the responsibility, liability and risk that they cover, but you also do not have the ability to make decisions that impact your own life ... or the lives of others.

Teaching others and seeing people succeed are two of my favourite things. I'm passionate about being a bridge-builder to help others achieve goals – and I'm really good at it, too.

Prior to the acquisition, my friends and other small business owners would often come to me for help starting their businesses or looking at processes and strategies for reinventing their struggling business. After doing this for a few years as a side-hustle for a few friends, those closest to me urged me to open my own business and start working to grow my own training company. That was a huge dream for me, and at the time, I wasn't used to dreaming that big for myself. I couldn't dream like that for myself because I was sowing into someone else's dream and putting all of my effort, all of my talent and all of my hard work into building someone else's business.

Sound familiar? Keep reading.

In 2017, I started my little training company. I say 'little training company' because at first, I just taught a few yoga classes and a couple of entry-level medical billing classes. As word got out about what I was doing, I began to receive more and more calls, and my company continued to grow and thrive – even though I was only putting my part-time effort into it.

I was a fearless leader when it came to running someone else's company, but when it came to leading my own business I struggled. I lacked confidence. I thought with a 'lack of' mentality. I flew under the radar and tried to hide and downplay my business and my abilities. I spent so much of my time trying to convince myself that I wasn't good enough to be an independent business owner that I nearly sabotaged myself completely! However, as the acquisition continued and as we started to transition to our new positions within the corporate world, I really felt like an outsider in the new company. The organisation I worked so hard to build was being dismantled right in front of me – slowly … and piece by piece. This was painful for me to watch; so painful that I began to withdraw from the position they had graciously allowed me to move into. I no longer had the ability to do good things for others and I had no impact on our business or our team. All I had to do was show up, punch the clock and go home. This did not work for me, and as hard as I tried to be a good employee, my spirit was broken. I was unhappy. I dreaded going to work each day and I just stopped smiling. It was this in the spirit of brokenness that the Lord catapulted me into my own business and started opening doors, windows and even breaking down walls to get me to new places and in front of new people. I often say I received a 'Holy push' to start sowing into my own business. By sowing into my own business, I would be able to make a positive impact once again on the personal growth and development of others. I could once again provide relevant work training and business strategy sessions to people who needed them. Being a person of faith, I surrendered to God's call on my life – the call to serve others in small business – and my confidence increased, my small business grew and my passion and joy for my work was restored!

That leads us to another tool that can help one become (and stay) successful in business: self-awareness. I would encourage you to take a self-inventory and begin to develop your personal leadership philosophy. Taking a self-inventory can help you understand more about yourself: your gifts, your talents, your skills, your work preferences and your habits. Before you strike out on your own into entrepreneurship, it's a good idea to know and understand a great deal about who you are and how you work, so you can assess all the 'pros and cons' of going into business for yourself. This also helps you better prepare when you're writing your business plan so you can have the best chance at success. I can't say enough about the importance of self-awareness and its relationship to continued success.

Once you've completed your self-assessment and you've determined that entrepreneurship is for you, then it is time to take action. You can't sit still and expect your situation to change. In order for there to be transformation in your life, you must take action! I would encourage you to simply start where you are. You may not feel ready to completely leave your nine to five right now, but there are steps that you can start taking toward starting your own business. Begin to seriously plan for transitioning to being your own boss. You'll need a business plan and a financial plan, but you'll also have a greater chance at success if you also develop an operational plan. This is the plan that directs not only *what* you do, but *how* and *when* you do it. Proper planning for your transition to entrepreneurship is a huge confidence-builder and can help you navigate the waters of uncertainty with a great sense of assuredness.

Here are the five simple rules that you can follow to maintain forward momentum and achieve excellence in your professional life:

1. Success is predictable; plan for it

Often, people are living with a misconception that a successful life is just a matter of luck or an accident. The same people are good at waiting for the miracles to happen in their life. They do not plan or strive to excel their abilities. In reality, success is predictable, and you can learn a particular set of skills to double, triple or quadruple your success rate. What you need to do is to watch how other professionals are planning their success and then adjust your strategies to ensure you get the same results. Seek help from someone you admire; read about them and plan like them. Follow their footprints and you will reach the same level of heights.

2. Put in the work with no excuses

What is self-discipline? It's the ability to dedicate your hours even when you don't feel like working. Successful people practice self-discipline rigorously. They avoid people who are lazy, procrastinate and are not courageous enough to reflect on which direction their life is heading.

I recently read a report that stated employees work for only three hours in their eight-hour job. Most of them waste their time gossiping about the movies, the kind of person they met last night at dinner and other subjects that are not relevant to their profession. You can easily beat 80% of the people around you by working for an extra hour or two in developing your skills rather than gossiping about politics and movies.

As Thomas Edison said, 'The three great essentials to achieve anything worthwhile are: hard work, stick-to-itiveness and common sense.'

3. Take control of the way you react

No profession is free from problems and challenges. The sooner you accept the truth, the better and easier it is for you to grow and excel your skills. Almost eight out of ten people do not have control over their reactions. When faced with a problem, they get angry and hold everyone responsible for leading the business in such a horrendous situation. They handle the situation irrationally and end up mounting more problems. How you respond to a particular situation determines how quickly you are going to climb up the ladder of your professional career. Luckily, like other habits, you can develop a strong – and positive – mental attitude while dealing with the problems.

4. Make results your priority

Instead of dwelling on the possibility of what you could have done to avoid the problem, think in terms of how you can mend the situation and bring out the desired result. High achievers do not play the blame game and are a part of those few personalities who set results as their topmost priority. To begin, embrace the situation as it is. Manage yourself in a way that no matter how difficult a particular situation seems, you're not going to accept the disappointments. Your response must be relaxed to every situation.

Practising such behavior over and over again automatically trains your mind to make the right decisions and lead you towards accomplishing the results you've desired. In the words of Jim Rohn, 'You must take personal responsibility. You cannot change the circumstances, the seasons or the wind, but you can change yourself. That is something you are in charge of.'

5. Look for something positive in every situation

The famous life coach Tony Robbins figured out that 'problems are the gifts that make us figure out who we are, what we're made for and what we're responsible to give back to life'. What an amazing thought that is! If you change your perception towards your problems and look at them as an opportunity to grow, then your life will immediately turn into an adventurous venture. All you have to do is pay attention to how you're talking to yourself and what kind of words you're feeding your subconscious mind.

Remember that 80% of our work and actions in day-to-day life are led by the guidelines of our subconscious mind. The surprising fact is that it's us who define these guidelines unknowingly. You cannot change the subconscious mind or cause at first, but you can always change its effect, and eventually how you react will automatically change the cause. Professional people are motivated people.

They plan their profession towards greatness and work hard even if they are not feeling like it. They're in control of how they react and look for the opportunities in every situation. They strive for superiority in their profession and make results their topmost priority.

If you really want to thrive in good times – and in times of adversity – one of the best ways I've found to do that is simply to be true to yourself. When you're working in your purpose according to the gifts that the Lord has given you – and in the way that He has called you to do it – you cannot fail. When an acquisition rocked my world and sent me into an ocean of uncertainty in my life, I was forced to re-evaluate the way I'd been living and the work I was doing.

The Lord opened doors for me, and I simply obeyed and walked through them. However, I was also planning and preparing as I went along so I would be ready to transition when the time was right. In all honesty, though, I was scared. I thought a corporate nine to five provided me stability and consistency, but while in the middle of an acquisition, I found out that when you work for someone else, you have absolutely no control over what happens to you; and things can change at any time. That realisation forced me to trust God more deeply and prepare myself more completely.

Whether you have a faith or not, is entirely up to you. You may choose an inspiration or a higher power that remains unnamed or unseen. However, through my belief in something bigger, I was challenged in ways that contributed to my success.

To be successful in life – and in business – I have also learned five things that helped me immensely. These are the lessons taught by positivity and planning in my professional life. I teach these to my clients, students and friends that come to me for career and business advice. This is what I share with them:

1. Know who you are and what you want.
2. Develop a plan to help you reach your goals.
3. Put in the work; no excuses.
4. Expect the unexpected. Things will always happen that will upset part of your plan, so be ready to go over, around or under things to continue moving forward.
5. Assess, celebrate, adjust and move forward regularly.

My message to those who feel stuck and as though you're struggling to get ahead in business is to simply be bold! Listen to the voice of positivity and drive the moves you forward; closer to achieving your goals and realising your dreams; closer to living the life that brings you the most happiness, fulfilment and joy! You can maintain momentum and excellence in your business by simply making a few adjustments in your planning, being consistent in the way you work and looking for opportunities to distinguish yourself from the pack.

You, too, can succeed!

SHEILA FARR

Sheila Farr is an eternal optimist! As the CEO of Gulf Coast Training & Education Services LLC, in Biloxi, Mississippi, she helps small businesses and entrepreneurs overcome obstacles and achieve their dreams by turning stumbling blocks into stepping stones. Sheila is a multi-time international bestselling author who loves to share strategies and tools that inspire and help people propel their careers – and their lives – to a new level. She's a cheerleader for others, inspires and motivates people through her blog, *Thankful and Blessed 365,* and is the founder of Biloxi Reads! – a literacy initiative along the Mississippi Gulf Coast.

ANNIE'S JOURNEY OF BECOMING

Annie Gibbins

Curiosity was my hobby

As I stood at the podium, with the lights pitching down either side of me, I could barely see the thousands of eager faces staring back. As I took a breath and smiled, there was one face I could see so crystal clear. Her face was proud. You could see her eyes slightly wider than usual, and her lips ever so slightly pursed in anticipation.

This poised, determined woman flicked her long brunette hair confidently over her left shoulder, and she nodded. This nod felt like she was the director, and I was an actor on stage, delivering the monologue in the final 'act'; the denouement of a show-stopping Broadway play. Holding herself confidently, this unnamed woman stood tall. Her red dress was tailored to perfection, and she smiled with her eyes, like she would to her children.

Fixed on her gaze, I tapped the tip of the microphone, making sure that every person in this imposing auditorium was prepared to catch my opening line. The silk-like silence did not intimidate me; in fact, I was the calmest I've ever been. I was ready. However, within seconds, the woman was gone. I blinked, and this fanciful figure had disappeared. It was then I realised there was no woman. There was no dreamlike, singled-out female. It was then I realised that this reflection was me.

I was the woman. *I* was the person who stood out so dreamlike and strong. For the first time in my life, everything made sense. In this moment, every baby feed, uni assignment, budget plan and career leap made complete and utter sense.

I was home.

'Good afternoon, my name is Annie Gibbins.'

Juggling babies & dreams

My grandmothers were my heroes. They were strong, resilient and unstoppable. However, life back then, some seventy years ago, was a very different landscape for women. There were no boardroom breakouts for both men and women. Back then, women would support the success of the man, and the woman's success was determined by the happiness and practical satisfaction of their spouse.

I am painting a very old-fashioned picture, but that was life. Men go to work; women keep the house. For women, ambition was measured by motherhood and domestic stature. For me, ambition was ranked by income, wealth and power. Sadly, there was no happy medium. Let's face it, even today, the disparity among men and women in business is alarmingly stark.

For me, my grandmothers oozed the qualities I wanted to inherit. I would mimic their boldness and ability to do it all. Whilst they were no financial moguls in the FTSE 500 Index, to me, they were everything.

When I was young, my heart's desire was to be a businesswoman.

I had seen men on TV, in magazines and on billboards, crossing arms and standing proud, commanding their companies' success. I was thirsty for the same. My mind was forever curious, and still is. I wanted to learn, read and translate every bit of knowledge I could get my hands and heart on.

I knew, unapologetically, I wanted fancy clothes, independence, a heavily stamped passport, freedom, confidence and money. It was glaringly obvious that these things were not going to get handed to me on a plate. The problem was – how?

Even now, I openly explain that my pathway to international business leadership was due to the right choices I made at the time. I backed myself and decided to pursue a less-than-conventional path. To this day, my life as a businesswoman, CEO, entrepreneur, board director and transformation coach was achieved by being one red-hot, formidable woman.

As we know, in business, you need a plethora of variables: purpose, planning, consistency, dedication and unquestionable tenacity. Yep, tick. Next? Sometimes a little luck. Let's be honest, whilst algorithms make most of our choices these days, so does a little dose of perfect timing.

At the tender age of twenty, I married my childhood sweetheart. Gosh, we were so in love, and remain besotted with each other today. Yes, I am one lucky girl, however, my marriage is a heart investment and I am one committed shareholder of our perfect love story. We knew we wanted a family so started planning straight away.

At twenty-three years old, I was pregnant with twins. Being pregnant for the first time is an incredible experience, but we were so happy. My husband and I are realists, and always have been. We knew we were going to be faced with the challenge of raising two babies when we had only planned for one, earning extra income and looking after two new humans as newlyweds.

Life was a struggle for the most part, but our tiredness was fuelled by love, and we knew how abundantly lucky we were. Knowing that we wanted a big family, less than two years later, I was pregnant again. I recall the look on our friends' faces. With two babies circling rings around us on a daily basis, for them, the idea of a third was a little crazy! But not for us – we were ready.

This is where the plot twist to our story took an unexpected turn. As both my husband and I sat down with our doctor for our routine ultrasound on pregnancy number two, what happened next you couldn't predict if you tried.

'Annie and James, you are having twins!'

This news left us speechless, speechless some more and in total shock. However, like anything in life, we took it by both hands and said, 'We can!'

Just twenty-six months after giving birth to twin boys, we welcomed a boy and a girl, and they were just perfect. Completing our family six years later, we welcomed our youngest daughter.

Life with twins is a job like no other, and trust me, I've juggled millions of dollars with a heavyweight board looking directly at me. However, this was hard; hard but perfect.

Women are powerful.

Something overlooked by so many.

Mothers often give this power away, not just to their children, but to others.

We forget to look after ourselves, we forget to dream and we forget to embrace the strength and capacity to achieve the extraordinary.

My children are my greatest teachers

Have you ever noticed how confident children are? They believe in amazing things like fairies and magic. Children have this innocent way of thinking anything and everything is possible. There is a fearlessness in a child's determination that makes me wonder if we tapped into our inner child more often, would we achieve more with the absence of ego and fear?

I adored my life as a mother of five, but because of, and not in spite of them, they made me tap into my self-belief. The belief that I felt as a child once, as I looked at my two grandmothers all those years ago.

I needed more. I wanted a big house in a nice suburb, nice clothes, family holidays and choices. I wanted to be in a position where I could work philanthropically and spend time giving back to the communities that need it.

As a young child, I was told that I didn't have the aptitude or the correct qualities to be a businesswoman. These statements and affirmations engraved themselves on my mind daily. So, despite not heading to business school, I did become a registered nurse and qualified with a Graduate Diploma in Nursing.

I adored this role. I adored learning and have always been curious about what does what, and how. Even if the information is not directly relevant to the task at hand, I need to know anyway.

The magic about determination and tenacity is that it will always find another way, and for me, it did. After years as a successful nurse, my duties were gradually being tapped into by departmental managers. Whilst my go-to thought back then was, *You won't go higher than this, Annie,* I desperately wanted to.

After all, my home life was no different to running a business. On an hourly basis, I was dealing with financial planning, budget cuts, conflict resolution and organisational structures, and if I could thrive as a mother, business would be the same.

The tables were turning

The day I became a nurse manager was a good day. For months and months, I would work shifts in the day and attend night classes in the evenings. My husband and I would juggle routines, regimes and feeding times. He was my biggest fan, and I would say the same today.

I was exhausted. Gosh, I won't say it was easy because it wasn't. Some days I would question why I was putting myself and my family through this organised chaos. However, that wasn't enough for me to stop. After graduating with a Master's of Education, I was overseeing the entire nursing department as the appointed head teacher.

You might guess what's coming next. Yes – I wanted more.

I knew my potential when some did not. Yet, what was scarier than not getting the next promotion or pitched deal was not trying at all. I knew who I wanted to be. I activated my curiosity and dared to dream bigger. I had the potential to be more, achieve more, earn more.

I heard on the job grapevine that there was a role coming for the position of national operations manager with Orthopaedic Surgeons of Australia. This esteemed organisation was seeking a health provider and educationist, who had a solid grasp of the health care system, and in particular, understood the ways surgeons tick (trust me, it's a thing).

Everyone I knew thought I was crazy! But me, I knew I was going to do this!

They would say, 'What about your kids? How are you going to deal with workloads and hours? How are you going to handle working with so many men? How are you going to cope? You've not done any formal business training so won't that go against you?'

Have you ever wanted to do something just to prove a point?

Well, I was making a point to myself and to them.

I thought, *What's the worst that could happen? If I have a chance of being exposed to an interview process, then surely that's growth potential?*

Close friends would say, 'We love your ambition, but you won't get the job with the competition you're up against.'

A week later, I got the job.

Why stop at enough?

Don't get me wrong, my close pal imposter syndrome came to give me their congratulations! Of course, I was concerned that I wasn't their 'typical' mould, but I used that to my advantage. I was always learning and never assuming. I was in the business playground, advising on national programs and heading up a multimillion-dollar budget. Anything I didn't understand, I would spend hours in my spare time learning. I was relentless in my pursuit for success, and my family backed me as I created my own path.

I was ecstatic, and life was incredible. I was in a beautiful marriage with my teenage love, I had five healthy children and I was finally a woman in business.

However … Can you guess?

Yes, I wanted more. Annie Gibbins needed to expand her knowledge, experience new challenges and find her next purpose. When a new CEO was introduced at the Orthopaedic Surgeons of Australia, I saw nothing outstandingly impressive. I thought to myself, *Annie, you could do that.*

Not every stepping stone in climbing the corporate ladder is going to be academic or deemed standard protocol. However, my journey was different, and that's okay. In fact, a different pathway is an attractive proposition to an organisation, and adaptability is everything in leadership.

Up for grabs was a CEO role with the Australasian Society for Ultrasound Medicine. I said to my friends (does this sound familiar?), 'I am going to apply to be the CEO for the Australasian Society for Ultrasound Medicine.' As I wasn't supposed to get the last job, what was the harm in putting myself forward against the odds?

In the job description, it was noted that they were seeking a health educationist that was capable of taking their national training programs to the next level. They wanted prestige, and I knew how to get them there. I prepped my heart out for the role. I created a 'my first one hundred days as CEO plan' and handed it out during the interview. To say they were impressed is an understatement.

I was the CEO for Australasian Society for Ultrasound Medicine for five years.

Hang on, I've made it

By my mid-forties, with five children, juggling the business, family and marriage, I was nailing my dream. However, after years in the not-for-profit sector, I wanted to sample a taster of the corporate sector.

After spending three years consulting, my skills were amping up and broadening out. My experience in C-suite roles was back to back, year to year. With the gift of comparison and a sustainable income, I felt it was time to head back to the charity sector. Within me is an innate desire to feel that levelling up and giving back go hand-in-hand.

It was time for me to step into my next role as CEO of Glaucoma Australia. I loved it. Every day, we got to help people save sight, and it felt so rewarding to be making such a personal impact. This incredible organisation's mission is to increase early detection and provide positive treatment outcomes through education, advocacy and research.

I knew as a child the leader I wanted to become, and I had achieved this. I was a confident CEO who knew how to cheer on a team, keep them accountable and deliver above expectations. It brought me pure joy to be positioned in my sweet spot.

For as long as I can remember, I will continually question my own heart's desire and the calling of my teams.

Do you have a desire to learn?
What are your natural gifts and talents?
What is actually driving you?
What is your passion and purpose?
What do I love ... empowering women?

As a global empowerment coach and keynote speaker, I am often asked, 'Why do you want to empower women?' In many ways, the answers seem obvious: to help, encourage and support. However, it's something bigger than that.

I grew up in an era where women were not encouraged to be successful, and other progressive women saw me as a competitor. After thirty years in business, I have learnt that there is enough business for everyone. When we collaborate globally, we will always enhance each other.

If you are good at what you do, you will shine! We don't need to be the best of everything. In fact, that's impossible if you want to lead. Be the best at leadership and great at the roles you manage but lead with your heart and never your ego.

I want to help women transform with my style and a pinch of magic that makes me, me.

We need skill, diversity, inclusion, versatility and most importantly, humility.

When I plunged myself into the digital pool of global networkers and leaders like myself, I created social and learning platforms designed for women like me. Annie, the woman who can. The woman who has worked tirelessly against the odds.

The three questions I ask when anyone asks to join The Women's Business Tribe:

How can we help?
How can I support you?
How can I empower you?

Nothing is impossible

During my last CEO tenure, I was tasked with finding the next patrons and influential ambassadors that would help to elevate our core message. So, not surprisingly, I started top down. I am not a woman who does life in halves! After months of kindly filling the inbox of the Governor-General of Australia, he agreed to come onboard. However, I didn't stop there. Over the next two years, I built key relationships with high-profile figures, and finally, music icon Kirk Pengilly from INXS and TV anchor David 'Kochie' Koch agreed to become ambassadors.

I was determined, honest and strategic. Their yeses came because I believed I could engage with two of Australia's public figures. You only ever achieve what you truly believe is possible. I needed to continue honing my skills until my clearly communicated pitch was met with, 'How could I not help you, Annie?' Now, millions more people are getting the message to save their sight, and what greater campaign for a CEO to champion.

Most things that matter take time, money, hard work and many iterations until the green light comes on and collective cheers erupt. But when reflecting back on a thirty-year career, I know one thing for sure: nothing is impossible. Every bit of magic can happen if you lean into your heart's desire and stay the course.

Life smashes the heart and soul of people because it can be brutal, not fair or equal. We don't all have a cheer squad in our arenas. So, when people don't take that next step, it upsets me because I know the next summit is possible for them to reach. As a hiker, life is a metaphorical (and literal) summit. I don't stop at the first peak. I inhale, observe, replenish and keep going. We can all learn how to do this.

I am acutely aware that strong desires can easily be quashed when doubt kicks in and confidence levels plummet. Juggling life as an entrepreneur can be a constant challenge, that's for sure. Navigating my own path to success, completing three university degrees around a large family and forging a career amidst male-dominated environments has been a mammoth task. But I strongly believe that when we enrich, learn and grow together, we thrive. Becoming the woman you were born to be is always worth your efforts.

I invite you to dream big, bold, scary, audacious goals and believe that nothing is impossible. Find your tribe, skill up, invest in you, back yourself even when others don't and be open to the wisdom of those who have successfully trodden the path before you.

Your world will then explode in all the right ways.

ANNIE GIBBINS

Starting her career as a registered nurse, Annie went on to become a health educationist, change management CEO and entrepreneur whilst raising her family of five, including two sets of twins born twenty-six months apart.

Annie Gibbins is a passionate and purpose-driven 'fempreneur', global women's empowerment coach, CEO, podcast host, speaker and number-one bestselling author.

Positioned as one of Australia's leading voices for women in leadership and founder of The Women's Business Incubator and The Women's Business Tribe, Annie is a digital powerhouse helping women push the limits of what is truly possible.

As G100 Australia Country Chair – Equity & Equality, her passion for gender equality is unwavering when it comes to excelling the potential of the female workforce. Annie is driven by demolishing the glass ceiling and removing the invisible barriers to success that many women come up against in their business and life journey.

As the host of *Memoirs of Successful Woman*, Annie has interviewed hundreds of inspirational women worldwide. Her continuous portfolio of high-calibre podcast guests range from business leaders, entrepreneurs, humanitarians, athletes and the creators of startups on a mission.

With three university degrees under her belt and twenty years of executive change management experience, Annie is now a go-to inspirational global speaker. In 2020, she earned the distinguished 'Unsung Business Hero' title in recognition of her formidable courage, compassion, perseverance, conviction and selflessness when coaching women to thrive. Speaking at the World Economic Forum, Annie shared the importance of engagement with political, business and cultural leaders to shape global, regional and industry agendas.

As a keynote speaker at the 'Lady America Power: Barriers and Bias, The Status of Women in Leadership' in 2021, Annie shared the power behind unlocking the visibility of female entrepreneurs around the globe. This prestigious event celebrated women internationally, heralding the importance of women in leadership.

Global brand, Hoinser Group, dedicated to promoting outstanding individuals in business throughout Europe, Africa, Asia, UAE and USA, invited Annie to their collective as an honourable member, elevating her influence tenfold.

Annie has graced covers and written articles for books and magazines including *1 Habit Leadership, I am Woman Global, Lady Speaker Power, Success, Hoinser, W, CIO Times,* and *MO2VATE Magazine.* She was named Top Women's Change Maker and Global Goodwill Ambassador in 2021.

www.ingramcontent.com/pod-product-compliance
Lightning Source LLC
Chambersburg PA
CBHW020316010526
44107CB00054B/1867